W9-CAI-106

Babywatching

Babywatching

Desmond Morris

CROWN PUBLISHERS, INC.
NEW YORK

Copyright © 1991, 1992 by Desmond Morris

All rights reserved. No part of this book may be reproduced or transmitted in any form or by any means, electronic or mechanical, including photocopying, recording, or by any information storage and retrieval system, without permission in writing from the publisher.

Published by Crown Publishers, Inc., 201 East 50th Street, New York, New York 10022. Member of the Crown Publishing Group. Originally published in Great Britian in different form by Jonathan Cape in 1991. CROWN is a trademark of Crown Publishers, Inc.

Manufactured in the United States of America

Library of Congress Cataloging-in-Publication Data
Morris, Desmond.
   Babywatching / Desmond Morris.
   Includes index.
   1. Infants. 2. Infants—Development. I. Title.
HQ774.M665 1992
305.23′2—dc20   91-43202
                                                           CIP

ISBN 0-517-58845-5

10 9 8 7 6 5 4 3 2 1

First Edition

Contents

Babywatching

Foreword
by Dr. Paula Elbirt Bender

Who are these babies, anyway? What do they want, what are they saying to us if anything at all? Is today's child a new breed? Scrutinized since before birth, our offsprings are in some regards less understood than ever. As we look less to our instincts and more toward intellectual achievement, we may have collectively deprived ourselves of the conventional wisdom of our ancestors. Expectation has replaced exultation and the parenting experience has been transmuted into an exercise in better-baby-building. Gone are the simple pleasures.

Gone, too, are our guideposts, discarded as restrictive and premodern and therefore no longer worthy of evaluation. Cornered by technology, today's parents, and many child-care professionals, are often clueless, caught in a babble of parenting techno-lingo. Woe to the parent who attempts the job with old-fashioned advice of parents, grandparents, or other vintaged authorities of former times.

Enter *Babywatching*; an objective, often playful, observational presentation; mostly descriptive, frequently analytic. Now we see the baby unveiled, unburdened by layers of societal dress. From this concise and poetically phrased work we can learn what to expect from the normal baby. We learn how to respond to a baby's subtle language, when and how to enter their private world and why parenting is a partnership affair, with a constant thrust toward change and adaption to challenge. These pages unfold the daily issues we face as mothers and fathers, caretakers and pediatricians, making sense of what has often been obscured by interpretation without thorough observation. Morris has more than done his homework for us. He has placed a key in the door and opened it for us. This volume invites us, coaxes us to see the simple beauty in our procreation. Our children will emerge freer, less constrained by faulty assumptions and perhaps with more self-esteem than previous generations.

Over years of experience as both a parent and a pediatrician, I have held many hands through everyday anxieties. These are about simple things: sleeping, not sleeping, crying, squirming, blinking, burping, bathing. Often these are the sorts of issues you wouldn't expect people to be pained by, but pained they are. My well-attended parent programs bulge with tension as issues of normal child behavior reveal the mass of misinformation parents have collected. *Babywatching* is long overdue. It is what we have been doing all along, baby watching, only blindly. This new guide should help us reach our goal of fostering happier, healthier families.

Introduction

I t is not exaggerating to say that the human infant is the most remarkable life-form ever to draw breath on this planet.

Small, vulnerable, and wordless though the baby may be, it is at the same time power-packed with astonishing potential. Programmed by a million years of evolution to transform its sophisticated parents into doting protectors, it radiates irresistible appeal. But how deeply do we understand its true nature?

How much do we really know about its behavior and its reactions to the world around it? Have we, perhaps, sometimes been misled by old traditions—entrenched ideas that tell us more about the adults that support them than they do about the babies themselves?

It is time to set the record straight, time to tear away the veils of superstition, fashionable distortion and adult-centered bias, and look again with an unprejudiced eye at the baby itself. This is not easy. They are such charmers that it is difficult to maintain an objective approach. One gurgling smile from a tiny face and even the hard-nosed scientist is undone. A special effort is needed to keep a clear head, but if this can be achieved some fascinating facts come to light, and a revealing new picture of the baby's world begins to emerge.

After studying human adults for many years, I have decided in *Babywatching* to focus my attention exclusively on the first twelve months of human life—the official period of babyhood, before walking and talking arrive on the scene. The subject may be familiar, but with an observer's eye I have tried to bring a new approach to bear on a number of the most intriguing and frequent queries:

Why, for instance, do human babies enter the world with such difficulty, when the young of other animals arrive so simply? And why do they cry so much more than the young of other species? How well can babies see, hear, smell, and taste? Close examination reveals that they are much more sensitive to the outside world than was once believed. How do they feed, sleep, dream, play, and crawl? Why do they alone weep, smile, and laugh? Just how intelligent are they? Can babyhood be rushed, or must events proceed at their own fixed pace? Is it true that newborn babies can swim under water? And can sleeping mothers really distinguish the cries of their own babies from those of others? Most important of all, how much love and comfort do babies need from their mothers?

In the past, adults have sometimes wrongly looked upon the baby as a "blank canvas" on which anything can be imposed, or as a little lump of insensitive flesh, barely reacting to the outside world except in a few very basic ways. One Victorian commentator summed up this condescending attitude with the remark: "Here we have a baby. It is composed of a bald head and a pair of lungs." In similar vein an insensitive priest defined a baby as "A loud noise at one end and no sense of responsibility at the other."

We now know better. In reality, the baby is highly responsive to its environment, right from the moment of its birth, and it is endowed with an immense capacity for stimulating its loving parents, and for monitoring and influencing their behavior.

Contrary to certain opinions, babies are almost impossible to train. Throughout their entire babyhood they only respond badly to attempts to chastise them or to over-regulate their lives. Unless their parents have been indoctrinated with inappropriate regimes, they will escape this fate. And so they should because a secure babyhood provides the basis for a successful adulthood. No baby can be loved too much.

Babywatching is a way of looking at infants so that we can see the world from their point of view instead of ours. The more we can think like a baby, the greater our chance of becoming good parents. This applies to fathers as well as mothers, and if the chapters that follow sometimes seem to ignore the father's role, this is only because in the past so much of our information has been gleaned from observations of maternal behavior.

Babies not only bring intense joy, they are also our genetic immortality. If we rear them well, it is they who will continue our genetic progress through time. Because of our spoken or unspoken awareness of this continuity, the arrival of a new baby is a profoundly rewarding experience, no matter how familiar the event may have become. As Charles Dickens once remarked: "Every baby born in the world is a finer one than the last."

This said, I must apologize for referring to the baby as "it" throughout the book. Some authors use "he" or "she," but both methods exclude half the babies in the world. The English language is awkward in this respect. One author tried to solve the problem by using "s/he," which was so obtrusive on the page that it ended up being irritating. So I have settled for the rather impersonal "it."

No insult to babies is intended, as I am sure the text that follows will confirm. After writing this book I have even more respect and admiration for that most extraordinary of all living things . . . the human baby.

How Do Babies
Enter the World?

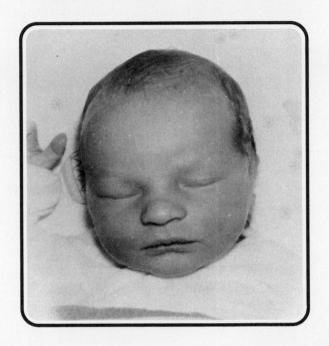

Often with great difficulty, as many women can testify. But why should human birth be such an effort, when so many other animals appear to produce their offspring with so little trouble? There is no ambulance to rush a mother giraffe to hospital when she is about to produce her six-foot-tall calf. Despite its ungainly shape, the newborn giraffe simply slides out of its mother's body, crashes to the ground and then quickly staggers to its feet. There are no doctors or midwives to assist an orangutan mother as her baby edges its way into the outside world. Again the whole procedure seems remarkably relaxed and simple. When the family cat hides away to deliver her litter of mewing kittens she does not appear to be racked with pain. She goes through birth after birth with quiet efficiency and little fuss. So why has the human baby's entry into the world become a time of such high drama and concerned medical supervision? Has our species become somehow inefficient at giving birth, and if so, why?

It is often argued that the frequent agonies of giving birth are the result of the fact that human beings, uniquely, spend their lives walking around on their hind legs. This bipedal position certainly puts some conflicting demands on the female pelvic girdle, which must be both a vertical locomotion support and a birth passage. The baby has to emerge through a ring of bone that must, of necessity, be a compromise between its two main functions. But although this factor may play a part in making human birth more difficult than birth in other species, it cannot be the whole answer for one very simple reason: primitive women did not have prenatal clinics, hospitals, drugs, anesthetics, and obstetricians for expectant mothers. The primeval human female had to produce her babies under simple, tribal conditions without any modern technology to help her, and she had to continue to do this for thousands upon thousands of years for our species to succeed. And succeed it did, on a global scale.

If primitive mothers could manage without any specialized help, why can we not do the same? A favorite answer is that the tribal mothers were working "in the fields" all day, and this made their bodies more muscular and stronger, so that they could give birth more easily. Bearing in mind how well fed we are today and how fit young women keep themselves, this explanation no longer seems very persuasive. It may have applied in epochs and cultures where women were made soft by being forbidden to do physical work, but even there it is hard to accept it as an important factor.

Looking at the evidence from ancient societies and from modern tribal societies in remote parts of the world, it seems that there are two major differences between their simple births and our more painful ones. These differences concern the *place* where the mother gives birth and the *position* in which she does it. We have altered these two aspects of delivery and, in doing so, have created unnatural obstacles to easy childbirth.

This may sound strange, but consider the facts. The tribal mother-to-be gives birth in a familiar place, soothed and helped by familiar female friends. She is not rushed off to a strange and rather daunting location, to be attended by strangers. The modern mother-to-be is not ill, but she is taken to a hospital—a place that we all automatically associate with sickness, injury, and pain. This removal to an unfamiliar place with alarming associations makes her anxious. Consciously, she knows that everything is being done to help her, but at a deeper, subconscious level, she feels the unease we all sense as we approach a hospital building.

This anxiety has a quite specific effect on her, and to understand it it helps to look at the behavior of certain other pregnant females. Among horses, the pregnant mare is capable of holding back her moment of delivery until she feels completely secure. Nine out of ten foals are born in the middle of the night. This is no accident, this is the result of the mares controlling the timing of their contractions. They wait and wait, until they are alone and all is quiet. Only then will they give birth. This is not something they learn. It is an instinctive ability and it helps the mother to make one of her most vulnerable moments also one of her most private.

This same mechanism is at work in humans. If the expectant mother is fearful or anxious, this mood automatically delays her labor. A specific chemical (epinephrine) is released into the mother's system and this has the effect of delaying the birth. The biological function of this postponement is, of course, to allow the mother to wait for a more relaxed, less intimidating moment before she becomes vulnerable. In primeval conditions this makes a great deal of sense. It helps her to avoid dangers. She can time her delivery to safer moments. But for the modern female it is no advantage at all. It is a nuisance. What is worse, the prolonging of the delivery makes her even more anxious and fearful and this in turn prolongs it still further. It is a vicious circle that sees many of today's mothers undergoing periods of labor many times longer than normal for our species.

This could be avoided if the mother felt entirely relaxed and "among friends." The less apprehension, the less pain. If mothers must be moved to maternity hospitals to give birth, for reasons of hygiene and access to medical emergency treatment, then those hospitals should be made as familiar and friendly as possible.

It has recently become fashionable for the father to be present at the birth. Although this is usually said to be a return to a "natural" condition of parental sharing, with the father's presence acting as a bonding device, the truth is that fathers do not seem to have been particularly prominent in the birth customs of ancient or tribal peoples. The supportive friends have almost always been exclusively female. Females who have previously given birth themselves seem to have been more calming in their influence than males. An "expectant father" may be even more anxious than the mother and risk transmitting his fears to her, worsening her state of mind instead of improving it. In other cases, however, the father is the only "body-intimate" a woman has today and so, in some instances, if he is calm and relaxed himself, he can provide the familiarity that she needs. It clearly depends on the individuals in each case.

From this argument it could be concluded that giving birth at home would be better. The mother would feel more at ease and the delivery would not therefore be delayed by internal chemical reactions to anxiety. This would be true if the home could be made hygienic enough and if the mother had around her expert, but familiar help. The problem for the modern female, however, is that she has been so firmly indoctrinated with the idea that it is only safe to go to hospital to give birth, that remaining at home might itself become a cause for anxiety. She is trapped between two alternatives, both of which have their own built-in anxiety factors: the hospital is strange and clinical; the home is lacking in expert technology. The solution must always be to choose the course of action that makes the individual mother feel most secure and relaxed.

Then she will not suffer the automatic "protection device" that is built in to her system and which keeps holding her baby back, no matter how hard she struggles to deliver it.

In addition to finding the right place to give birth, there is also the question of adopting the right posture for the delivery. If, again, we look at ancient and tribal societies, it is clear that lying down on your back to give birth is not the favored position. In fact, looked at logically, it is rather ridiculous, because it makes no use of gravity. Instead of "dropping" her baby, the mother has to be urged to "push, push." She must force the infant out horizontally. Again, this seems a strangely medical procedure that has no place at a "natural" event. It is as if the mother, having been shipped to hospital, is now being treated as though she really is ill. She is placed in a bed, like a patient, and attended by medical staff, as though there is something wrong with her—when in reality there is something wonderfully right with her. It seems as though this medically dominated atmosphere has been accepted as the inevitable norm for human mothers, but the truth is that it is no more than a modern fashion.

A survey of birth postures in tribal and ancient societies reveals that squatting, not lying, is the natural delivery position for our species. Even the ancient Egyptian hieroglyphic for "birth" shows a squatting woman with a baby's head emerging from below her body. The same is true in ancient Babylon, Greece, and in the Pre-Colombian peoples of Central America. In ancient Rome they made use of special birth chairs. These chairs had cut-away seats that permitted the baby to emerge downward while the mother clung on to handles fixed to the front of the chair arms. These devices remained popular in Europe for centuries and were still in use in some regions right up to the beginning of the twentieth century.

Giving birth in this way is easier, as we know from careful modern studies by anthropologists in New Guinea and elsewhere. Their observations of the few remaining tribal societies that have not yet been "helped" by advanced cultures, show that the primeval squatting position greatly reduces the effort needed to deliver the baby. There may still be contorted facial expressions and moments of inevitable discomfort and even pain, but the whole process is quicker and more efficient.

We need to relearn some old lessons when bringing babies into the world. Providing mothers are healthy and there are no signs of complications, we could do well to reconsider both the place and the position for delivery. Birth is a natural process and we should give biology as well as medicine due consideration when planning it.

Why Do Babies Cry When They Are Born?

Parents can be forgiven for smiling when they hear the first sounds of crying from their newborn baby. It signals to them that the new arrival is alive and breathing. But is this crying really necessary? At any other time it is a signal that distresses the parents and makes them anxious about the pain or discomfort they know the baby must be feeling. Is their joy at hearing the audible signs of life from their offspring masking what should perhaps more correctly be their concern about the baby's panic? Is the traditionally accepted procedure, at the moment of birth, the best from the baby's point of view?

To find the answer to this question we need to examine what confronts the baby as it emerges into the outside world. It comes from a warm, dark, quiet, soft, all-embracing, liquid world into one of stark contrast. In the old established hospital routine, there are bright lights—for those attending the birth to see clearly what is happening; there is considerable noise as the hospital staff encourage the mother and talk to one another; and, for the baby, there is loss of body contact as the doctor or midwife holds and examines it following delivery. Again, it has been a hallowed tradition for the doctor to slap the baby to encourage it to cry, as a way of initiating breathing. The ever-present fear that the baby may not start breathing quickly enough causes impatience and a deliberately harsh treatment to force the baby to react. Other procedures, such as cutting and clamping the cord, weighing and examining the infant, and washing and clothing it, may all be undertaken without delay as part of this standard medical sequence.

Like the parental smiles at the sound of crying, these hospital activities are easy to understand. The primary concern of the medical staff is that nothing should go wrong and that they should ensure for the parents the delivery of a physically sound and healthy baby. Nobody can blame them for this, but it has recently been suggested that, in their urge to ensure physical well-being, they have perhaps gone too far, treating the newborn as a patient instead of a perfectly healthy new arrival. In rare cases where there are genuine medical problems they are, of course, entirely justified with their speedy, businesslike approach, but in such instances they are today usually well aware of possible dangers before the delivery begins. The warning signs will have shown up during earlier examinations and they can then be ready for them. In the vast majority of cases, however, where both mother and baby are physically strong, healthy and normal, there is something to be said for a gentler, calmer approach to ensure that the baby is given the smallest possible trauma as it first encounters the outside environment.

What should this softer approach be? It is to proceed more gradually, so that the newborn can take on board the inevitable shocks of the outside world little by little, instead of in one dramatic explosion of novel stimulation. Observing the behavior of newborn babies closely soon reveals ways in which this can be achieved without taking any undue medical risks.

First, there is no need for loud voices or the clatter of hospital equipment once the baby has started to emerge. Unless something goes wrong with the delivery, the birth room can be kept completely quiet and the baby's ears can become slowly accustomed to the clamor of the open air.

Second, the bright lights of the typical hospital room can be dimmed considerably without serious risk, especially from the moment that the baby has been successfully delivered. Instead of screwing up its eyes against the glare it can then gradually adjust to this totally new sensory experience.

Third, its panic at loss of body contact can be much reduced by allowing it to remain in direct touch with its mother's body as it emerges. It is not held up, away from the mother, but placed gently on her stomach and left there to lie quietly in contact with her soft, warm skin. At the same time, adult hands can clasp and embrace it, holding it snugly on to the mother's body. Initially, these can be the hands of the doctor or midwife, but then the mother herself can take over and, for the first time, feel her baby's tiny shape. The change for the newborn from total contact to loss of contact is made into a gradual process instead of a sudden shock.

Modern doctors introducing this more gentle approach to birth have been rewarded with far less panic-stricken newborn babies. There are no screaming, contorted faces. The new arrivals lie placidly and peacefully in their mother's arms, calmly resting after their strenuous journey. They may not be totally silent but the expected prolonged screaming is replaced by no more than a few brief cries as they emerge from the birth canal. These cries are the inevitable consequence of the sudden expansion of their small chests as they leave the tight constriction of the vagina. One moment their chests are compressed and the next they are expanded and this encourages the air to rush in. The exhalation that follows produces the brief crying sound, but this is quickly followed by silence if the newborn's body is kept in contact with the mother and moved gently up to lie on her.

At this point there is a moment of peace and rest for both baby and mother. Instead of hurrying on with the various medical procedures—cutting the cord, washing, weighing, and clothing the newborn—it is left in its mother's embracing hands to adapt to its new world. There really is no urgency at this stage. The cord continues to beat for several minutes after a normal birth and still provides the vital oxygen supply from the mother to her infant. While this is happening the baby will start to breathe with its own lungs, little by little replacing the old system with the new. Hurrying to cut the cord does nothing to help the baby and only forces it to switch to lung breathing with extreme rapidity, once again putting a sudden strain on the newborn. The gradual approach allows the arrival of lung breathing to occur at the baby's pace, rather than the hospital's.

As far as washing, weighing, and clothing the baby is concerned, this can all wait. The baby's body is covered in a protective layer of grease beneath which its skin is tender and extremely sensitive. Contact with its mother's soft stomach and hands is far kinder than with towels and clothing. Again, the slow approach favors the baby and gives it time to settle and adjust.

Something else important is happening, too, and that concerns the mother. Instead of having her newborn whisked away from her immediately, she is able to feel it with her fingers and, in the key moments of her reproductive experience, to relish its presence. This is a climactic moment and she should not be cheated of it by over-efficient professionals—with what could be described as a *partus interruptus*. A normal birth is not a surgical operation, it is a moment of supreme biological importance during which the medical atmosphere should always be kept in a subordinate role unless an emergency occurs.

In peace and quiet, in a dim light, unhurriedly, the mother can then come to terms with her baby's existence. Eventually, when the shock of the delivery is past, for both parent and child, the usual procedures can be carried out. Before this is done, however, the baby can be gently shifted up to the mother's breast where it may start to suck straight away. This move also permits the mother to take a close look at her new arrival as she cradles it in her arms. This is a stage that helps to tighten the bond even more than usual. And it can surely not be an accident that the average umbilical cord is just long enough to permit the newborn to be put to the breast while it is still attached to the placenta.

Unless the delivery has been abnormally exhausting, both mother and baby will be wide awake during the moments that follow. During the first hour of its life, the baby's eyes are nearly always open and the face-to-face contact that can follow the delivery is something that should not be curtailed for any mother who wants it. Eventually the cleaning-up can begin, but even then the baby should be returned to the mother's embrace at the earliest possible moment. The traditional hospital regime saw the baby taken away to a remote nursery cot, alongside rows of other babies. Each baby was then taken to its mother every four hours for regular, regimented feeding sessions. This was a totally unnatural procedure and certainly one that no tribal mother (or chimpanzee for that matter) would tolerate. Unless the mother is ill or seriously incapacitated in some way, she should be separated as little as possible from her baby during these early days.

It may be argued that this is no more than a call for a romantic "return to nature" and that, in terms of modern child welfare, it has no value. There is convincing evidence against this criticism. Back in the 1970s some astute observers carried out detailed studies of newborn babies with their mothers. One group of mothers experienced the usual hospital routine and a second group were allowed an additional five hours a day of cuddling-contact with their babies. After they had all left the hospital, the observers did some follow-up checks on their later behavior. They discovered that, one month after the three-day hospital stay, the "cuddling-contact" mothers displayed more body intimacy in dealing with their babies than those that had undergone the traditional hospital routine. They embraced them more warmly when feeding them and indulged in more eye-to-eye contact. A year after the three-day hospital stay, the "cuddling-contact" mothers still showed some differences, remaining closer and more protective whenever their infants showed any signs of discomfort or distress.

Clearly, prolonged contact during the first crucial days of maternity is important in strengthening the parent-offspring bond. It would, however, be foolish to claim that it is essential. Many babies survive well enough without such contact, but if it can be offered to a mother without causing any problems, then it seems foolhardy to eliminate it simply because of some long-standing tradition of hospital procedure.

Recently certain French doctors have introduced extreme measures for "naturalizing" the birth of babies, employing near-darkness, almost complete silence, and a reverently gentle laying-on of hands with the newborn. The results have been spectacular in terms of newborn calm and comfort, but a new kind of panic can be caused if the process is taken too far. Some of the mothers became alarmed at the almost too-peaceful atmosphere. Having been brought up to expect noise, bustle, and clatter at the scene of the birth, they feared that some sort of disaster must have occurred and that their so-quiet babies must be dead or dying. Such is the conditioning to which whole generations have been exposed. In some cases it was hard to convince them that their babies were performing normally and naturally. Clearly there is no advantage in taking the process so far that the panic eliminated from the newborn is switched to the mother. Both should be as calm as possible for the magic of the early bonding between mother and child to take effect. This can be done by a carefully balanced compromise between the expected traditions and the more patient approach of the "biological delivery."

The presence of fathers during and after the birth has a similar bonding effect. If they take time to hold, cuddle, and rock their babies during the first few hours after birth, they too remain closer to them later on. It is no accident that human babies remain awake during the first hour or so of their lives, before falling into a long, deep slumber. During this waking period they are more alert than they will be for several days and this special level of activity may have evolved quite specifically as a "bonding time," the active baby transmitting signals of enormous appeal to its parents at a time when they themselves are in a highly emotional condition. This powerful combination, it would seem, plants deep roots of love into the family unit.

Why Is the Newborn Covered in Grease?

At first sight, the newborn human baby fresh from the womb is reminiscent of a swimmer about to attempt the English Channel. What the two have in common is a thick covering of whitish grease giving them a strange pasted look. For the swimmer the grease acts as a thermal barrier. For the infant there may be a similar advantage after the delivery is over, the extra coating helping to buffer the newborn against any sudden drop in temperature, but its main function comes earlier, as a lubricant.

Technically the grease is known as the *vernix caseosa* which means literally the "cheesy varnish." It is formed from a mixture of shed flakes of skin and oily secretions from the sebaceous glands. These glands, which are associated with hair follicles, become unusually active in the last few months of pregnancy, so that by the time of birth they have coated the whole surface of the baby's body with a slippery layer that eases its passage through the tight birth canal. Without it, birth would be almost impossible.

An additional function suggested for the vernix is that it helps the skin of the unborn baby to resist water-logging as it floats in the amniotic fluid, but if this is the case, it is surprising that it is only fully developed in the final weeks of the nine months pregnancy. Its special timing strongly favors the lubrication theory.

A secondary function that is more convincing is its role as a defensive barrier against minor skin infections during the vulnerable first few days of life. For this reason, it is sometimes left in place until it falls away naturally, about two or three days following delivery.

For many mothers, however, the idea of having a new baby caked in what has been described as a "cream cheese pack" is slightly offensive and there is a strong urge to have the infant washed clean as soon as possible. This is, indeed, the favored routine in most places, after which the baby is gently wrapped in soft warm clothing. Given the high levels of hygiene that have become common practice with the newborn today, the risk of increasing its vulnerability to infections because of this cleansing is minimal.

How Soon Does
the Navel Heal?

The umbilical cord that attaches the baby to its mother's body grows longer and longer during pregnancy until about the twenty-eighth week. Then its growth stops, regardless of how long it may be at the time. Surprisingly its length is highly variable, but we have no idea why this should be. In fact, it is just about the most variable feature of the baby, the "normal" range of lengths being between a mere 7 inches and an impressive 48 inches. The average is about 20 inches. The dimensions of the mother's body and that of her baby's have no influence on the length of the cord. There is only one feature that does show any relationship to cord length and that is the baby's gender. The cords of male babies, for some unfathomable reason, are on average about 2 inches longer than those of female babies.

When the baby is born the cord is still beating, blood being passed at four miles an hour through its one large vein and its two arteries, providing the baby with oxygen and nutrients. This continues for about five minutes. Then, when the beating has stopped, the cord is clamped in two places and severed between them. The stump that is left protruding from the baby is usually about 2 to 3 inches long and a plastic clip is attached between its severed end and the place where it enters the baby's body, at a point that is about half an inch to an inch away from the body surface. This clip stays in place until the stump dries off, shrivels, and falls away.

When the baby is born the cord has a strange bluish-white color, but as it starts to dry it darkens and blackens. This happens within a few hours. The time it takes to drop off is between five and ten days.

Once the stump has dropped away it leaves a "raw" navel exposed to the air, which soon hardens. At this stage the navel protrudes slightly. In some babies it protrudes to an alarming degree, but as time passes it gradually flattens. Even if there is a slight hernia (which is common), there is no real danger, although this may take some months to disappear.

None of these stages is painful to the baby. The whole process is part of the natural shift from the attached to the unattached condition. It needs little help from the mother and the general rule is "leave well enough alone." The important point to remember is that, in the primeval state, the navel would not have been covered up, taped, or strapped up. It would have been exposed to the air. It needs to be clean and, above all, dry. If it is wet or moist, the natural drying-out process cannot proceed properly. It is best left uncovered as much as possible to allow this to take place speedily.

We may think of this procedure of cutting the cord within a few minutes of birth as ancient and traditional but in reality it has only been in general practice for a few hundred years. Before that it was more usual to await the delivery of the afterbirth—the placenta. Recently in Hungary there has been a return to this earlier method, for a special reason. Doctors there pointed out that, when birth occurs, part of the baby's blood is inside the cord and the tissues of the placenta, and that by waiting for the afterbirth, it is possible to give the newborn its extra ration of blood. The method they adopt is to keep the baby lying on the mother until the placenta is delivered, which takes between fifteen and thirty minutes. The placenta is placed in a dish and held up in the air, above the level of the baby. The blood in the placental tissues can then drain down the cord and into the baby's system. This can increase the baby's blood volume by as much as 25 percent and gives it an extra boost as it starts on its new life. Even without going to these extremes, it is possible to boost the baby's blood appreciably simply by waiting the five minutes it takes for the cord to stop pumping, instead of cutting the cord immediately after delivery.

A final point about the fate of the cord. Today we simply throw it away as "hospital waste," but this too is a very recent procedure. In tribal societies the cord was thought of as vastly important for a variety of magical reasons. It was often ceremonially eaten as a medicine, buried, worn, or placed in a tree. In many tribes it was carried as a lucky charm and in other cultures it was sometimes carefully preserved in the family archives and was then ritually entombed with its owner when he or she died. In modern times we are more matter-of-fact with it, discarding it casually the moment its task has been completed.

Why Do Babies Yawn When They Are Born?

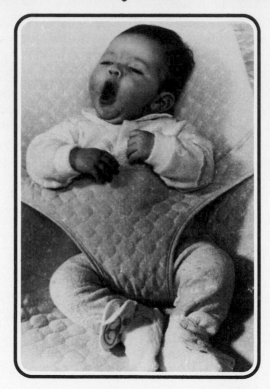

U nder natural circumstances, the newborn baby gives a few massive yawns shortly after it has been delivered. Considering its exertions during its long struggle to leave its mother's body, it would seem reasonable to suppose that it is yawning because it is tired, but this is not the real explanation. The huge birth-yawns are reflex actions that ensure a deep intake of oxygen to the lungs.

This is crucial at the very start of the baby's independent life outside the mother's body.

For many modern babies, this primeval yawning is obliterated by medical practice. If the birth process is hurried and the baby handled in such a way that it cries intensely, the birth-yawns are eliminated. If, on the other hand, the birth sequence is taken at a more leisurely pace, and the umbilical cord is left attached for several minutes, the baby is able to start breathing in its own good time, yawning as it does so. This breathing and yawning process begins naturally, long before the cord switches off its supply of maternally oxygenated blood. But in the anxiety of supervising the drama of birth, patience is a virtue that often eludes those who are present. The fear that the baby may not breathe at all is so great that the whole process is rushed and the baby is forced to switch on its breathing system more rapidly than nature intends.

Where more thoughtful and experienced helpers are at hand, or where birth takes place in more "primitive," less clinical conditions, however, the newborn's act of yawning is commonly observed and from it has sprung a curious custom that most of us still follow throughout our adult lives—the custom of covering our mouths with our hands when we yawn. Today we describe this simply as "good manners," but we never say quite why this should be. We often "expose" our open mouths at other times when it is not considered to be bad manners, so why should yawning be singled out in this way?

The answer lies in a false association between the yawning of newborns and a high mortality rate among babies. Needless to say, infant mortality has nothing to do with the yawning at birth—just the opposite in fact—but the link was made by superstitious minds many centuries ago. It was thought that, when the babies opened their mouths wide in the act of yawning, they were letting a part of their soul escape from their bodies and that this so weakened them that they soon died. So many babies did indeed die in the first days and weeks of life (largely because of poor hygiene and other damaging birth practices) that it was natural to seek some sort of explanation. If the explanation exonerated those who were responsible for the poor conditions that led to early deaths, so much the better. What better than to blame the great yawning actions of the newborn? In ancient Rome, mothers were advised to watch carefully for any signs of yawning in their babies and to cover their mouths whenever possible, to stop the repeated "weakening" of the infant's soul that would result from these dangerous actions. As soon as the infant had reached an age where it could cover its own mouth it was instructed to do so, and it was this practice that survived into adulthood and also into modern times.

So today, when we cover our mouths as we yawn, we are—without realizing it—reenacting the ancient custom of keeping our souls inside our bodies. What we describe as merely polite is in reality rooted in primitive superstition.

Why Are Some Babies Born Hairy?

Occasionally when a baby is born it is found to be almost completely covered in a soft, downy coat of hair. This sometimes horrifies the new mother, who has the fantasy that she has given birth to a tiny, furry ape instead of a beautiful bouncing baby. In reality she has no need for concern. All she is seeing is a slightly delayed fetal condition. It will soon pass, usually in only a few days. In exceptional cases it has lasted as long as four months after birth, but it always fades away in the end, to reveal the smooth naked skin that every mother expects.

This rare covering of newborn body hair should not therefore be a cause for horror or revulsion, but should be looked upon as an unusual opportunity to gain a fleeting glance of what *every* baby looks like during its final weeks in the womb. For this woolly coat of down is found on all babies in the final months of pregnancy. It is called the *lanugo* (which literally means wool). The word was originally used to describe the fuzz on a peach, before being borrowed by human medicine.

The lanugo's earliest appearance on the developing fetus is during the fifth month of pregnancy, but it is more likely to arrive in

27

the sixth month. It starts to disappear in the seventh month and is nearly always gone by the eighth. In some babies it lingers until the ninth month, vanishing just before birth. In a few, rare instances it survives birth and displays itself to the startled parents.

Some hairy babies are only partially covered with this lanugo. In their case it is usually the shoulders and back that are affected. With others, the cheeks and ears are also involved and in a few the whole surface of the body is downy, with the exception only of the palms of the hands and the soles of the feet. This exception is significant, for in hairy mammals, these are often the only naked-skinned parts of the body. In other words, this exception underlines that what we are seeing in the lanugo is a brief reminder of our ancient ancestry. It confirms what biologists have believed for years, namely that mankind evolved from hairy mammalian ancestors and is part of the great primate evolutionary picture. There is nothing shameful about this. We should be proud of our animal ancestry. Our animal qualities are among our most laudable. It is among our uniquely human qualities that we find our worst traits.

What are the chances of having a hairy baby? Very small, unless the baby is premature, in which case they are high, because, of course, the preterm newborn is emerging at the stage when most babies are still in the normal lanugo stage. Certain abnormal conditions also increase the chances of a hairy baby. Under the influence of cortico-steroid drugs, in cases of hypothyroidism, and where babies are severely malnourished, the newborn is more likely to emerge into the world clad in its silky soft, downy, woolly lanugo.

A possible explanation of the timing of the lanugo is that its sudden growth spurt may be associated with the formation of the greasy covering of the fetus, the *vernix caseosa*. In a typical baby, the lanugo appears first and then the greasy layer, during the final months of pregnancy. The grease arises from the sebaceous glands which are connected with the hair follicles. It may well be that, as these glands become more active, the hair follicles are automatically activated with them, creating the woolly covering. Having done its job, the woolly coat then disappears before birth, leaving only the greasy layer as the vital lubricating medium for the process of delivery.

What Are the Baby's Vital Statistics?

Babies vary a great deal at birth, but it is useful to know what the average human baby is like.

The typical baby is born after a gestation period of between 252 and 293 days. Anything less is a premature baby, anything more is overdue. The most likely time period between the act of fertilization and birth is 266 days. A popular alternative way of measuring the long wait for the baby's arrival is to say that it will be 280 days after the last menstrual period—something that can often be calculated more accurately.

For some reason we do not understand, female babies on average spend a day longer inside their mother's bodies than their male counterparts. And white babies on average spend five days longer inside than black babies. In India, the average gestation period is even longer, Indian babies spending six days more inside their mothers than typical white babies. These differences are purely racial and have nothing to do with the size of the babies, or the affluence or poverty of the families concerned. To date, nobody has been able to offer any explanation for these puzzling variations.

The baby's best chance of surviving gestation and of experiencing a trouble-free birth is when the mother is somewhere between the age of eighteen and thirty. The very best age of all, from the newborn's point of view, is when the mother gives birth at the age of twenty-two. This is the age of fecundity for human females, with fetal deaths down at the very lowest rate of only twelve per 1,000. By the time the mother has reached the age of forty-five, this figure has risen to forty-seven deaths in every 1,000.

The oldest woman to successfully give birth was fifty-seven years old. This is highly unusual, however, the average age for the female menopause being fifty-one.

At birth, the typical weight for a human baby is 7½ pounds (3,500 grams). There is considerable variation, but only 5 percent of babies fall outside the range of 5½ to 9½ pounds (2,500 to 4,250 grams). The average male weighs ½ pound more than the average female. The birthweight shows a slight decrease during the first three days after birth, losing about one tenth of its original figure. This is perfectly normal and is part of the readjustment to life in the external world. After a further week has passed, the lost weight has been regained, as the long-term growth process asserts itself. During the first month of life outside the womb, the baby will, on average, put on 7 ounces (225 grams) each week. At the age of five months, the baby will have doubled its birthweight and at the end of babyhood, when it has reached the age of one year, it will be three times as heavy as it was when it was born.

A newborn baby's height is slightly less than one-third of that of the typical human adult. The average figure is 20 inches (51 centimeters), with all but 5 percent of babies falling within the range of 18 to 22 inches (46–56 centimeters). By the end of babyhood, at twelve months of age, its body height will have increased by 10 to 12 inches.

The human brain, already huge by animal standards, more than doubles its weight in the first twelve months of life outside the mother's body. When the baby is born it is a quarter of its adult weight and by the end of the first year it is up to 60 percent.

At birth, the head is huge in relation to the rest of the body. The height of the head of the newborn is 25 percent of its total body height. This ratio shrinks as the baby develops until, with human growth finally completed, the head represents only one-eighth of the total adult height.

The newborn heart weighs less than an ounce, but by the end of the first year has grown to 1.6 ounces in weight. The pulse rate averages 140 beats per minute during the early weeks of life, falling to 115 by the end of the year. At the time of the birth it is exceptionally high—as much as 180 beats per minute, it then falls to a much lower level within a few hours.

The vast majority of boys have fully descended testicles at birth (98 percent), and within the first month of life most of the remaining babies will follow suit.

Chemically, the newborn baby's body is made up of roughly 70 percent water, 16 percent fat, 11 percent protein, and 1 percent carbohydrate.

Why Does
a Baby Have
a Soft Spot
on Its Head?

W e think of the hard, bony human skull as a valuable piece of protective armor for the delicate brain inside—a biological crash helmet. In which case, why is the new baby's skull so soft? With the newborn's weak neck and clumsy body, it would seem that the need for a strong crash helmet was immense and yet at its most vulnerable time the young human brain appears to be in its most exposed condition.

The answer lies in the adoption of a vertical posture by our species countless thousands of years ago. When the human female stood up on her hind legs and started to walk bipedally, she put new demands on her pelvis. Her shape had to be a compromise between the old needs of giving birth and the new needs of vertical locomotion. The result was a rather restricted birth canal through which the baby had to pass to enter the outside world. To achieve this passage the newborn was forced to become streamlined. A broad, stiff skull would be too blunt a leading edge for the head-first exodus from the womb. A modified design was needed—one with a more tapered point. But how could the young skull be improved in this way?

First, the growing skull bones had to be softer and more pliable. Second, they had to be in separate plates rather than in one complete bony sphere. And third, they had to be able to move slightly in relation to one another and even overlap with one another if necessary.

These special qualities gave the newborn, as it started to plunge down the narrow vaginal passage, a slimmer, more flexible shape that was much easier to squeeze into the outside air. At their soft edges, the bony plates of the skull could slide over one another and briefly make the head more pointed than normal. Some mothers are alarmed to find that, as a result of this remarkable piece of human engineering, their baby has arrived in the world with a lopsided or elongated skull. They immediately fear some kind of defect or abnormality, but their fears are without foundation. The skull has an impressive ability to correct its shape and symmetry within a few days. At worst, the remolding of the skull only takes a few weeks. The exact time depends on the tightness of the vaginal passage and the difficulty experienced in delivery. Usually the skull distortion is greatest with first-time mothers. After each birth, the problem becomes a little easier, the pressure on the baby's head a little less.

So the protective factor had to give way to the ease-of-delivery factor, when considering the design of the infantile skull. The crash helmet proper had to wait until the child was older. In the earliest weeks and months, protection had to be delegated to the mother. But given this valuable flexibility, the young skull would have to possess special growth patterns, unique to its variable shape.

Initially the newborn's skull is made up of several curved plates separated by membranous gaps where the edges of the bones do not fit snugly together. It is these gaps that allow the head to distort as it passes through the canal at birth. The spaces are filled with soft but tough fibrous tissue. At six points the gaps between the bones widen out to form larger, *soft spots* called *fontanelles*. The reason for this name, which literally means "little fountain" is that the softness of the spots gives the impression that liquid could suddenly well up through them. Certainly, the new mother touching one of these soft spots for the first time is quite alarmed at what seems to be a desperately delicate patch on her baby's head. Again her fears are unfounded. The membranous tissue that covers them is extremely strong and resistant to all damage except a direct, sharp blow.

The six fontanelles are not all of the same size. There are two main ones and four minor ones. The main ones are on top of the head—the anterior fontanelle, just at the top of the forehead, and the posterior fontanelle, at the rear of the top of the head. The anterior is the bigger, but its size is very variable. At its smallest it is no larger than the tip of the mother's finger when she presses it gently. At its largest it can be between 1 and 2 inches across. It is roughly diamond shaped, although to the cautious touch it usually feels more or less circular. The slightly smaller posterior fontanelle is triangular in shape.

The four minor soft spots are the paired anterior lateral fontanelles and the paired posterior ones. These are positioned below the temples and low down at either side of the rear of the skull.

Some mothers imagine that there is a cranial defect when they can see the baby's pulse beating visibly through the major, anterior fontanelle at the top of the center of the forehead. This pulsing is quite normal, but it is more worrying if the soft spot is hollow or bulging. If hollow, it indicates that the baby is feverish or dehydrated and urgently needs liquid nourishment. This sometimes happens in very hot climates and also during certain illnesses. If the soft spot is strongly convex, then there is something seriously wrong, but this is extremely rare.

During the first two months of life outside the womb, the fontanelles enlarge slightly as the skull starts to grow. As this happens the fibrous tissue between the bony plates begins to harden and ossify. The edges of the plates spread out toward one another until they touch, meeting in wavy lines that fit together like the pieces of a human jigsaw. These wavy lines, called sutures, become cemented together more and more powerfully as the skull hardens and strengthens. As the months pass the fontanelles shrink and eventually disappear. The crash helmet has been perfected. It still has to grow, however, and it does this by laying down more bone on its outer surface and losing layers of bone on its inner surface.

All through childhood it expands gradually in this way until, at adolescence, the adult size has almost been reached. All bone growth finally ceases in the young human being at the age of about twenty-five years.

The length of time it takes for the soft spots to become hard varies enormously from infant to infant. They have been known to disappear as early as four months and as late as four years. The big anterior fontanelle on the top of the forehead usually takes the longest—typically between eighteen and twenty-four months. The posterior and the small lateral fontanelles are usually closed over in less than a year—sometimes in only a few months. Early or late closing does not seem to mean anything in particular and nothing can be read into variations of this kind. Nor need parents worry too much about the supposed delicacy of the soft spots before they have ossified. The membranes covering them are strong and tough and ordinary washing and rubbing in these areas do no damage whatever.

Another parental anxiety often arises when the young mother observes that one side of her baby's head is flatter than the other, even some months after the birth. Although this is not common, it does occur in quite a number of babies and is caused by the development of a very early sleeping habit in which the infant always places its head on the surface of its cot or bed in exactly the same way every time it goes to sleep. The bones of the head remain remarkably pliable during these early months, even while the soft spots are hardening over, and by lying always in the same posture the babies tend to flatten out the area that happens to be the habitual "underside." This creates a lopsided head with what is sometimes called a "parallelogram skull." Attempts to lay the baby in different sleeping postures sometimes succeed, but babies are quite capable of abandoning these new resting postures and stubbornly returning to their favored position as soon as they are left alone. Even so, there is no cause for concern. Although the lopsidedness may increase for some months it will eventually disappear and, by the time the infant is two or three years old, the skull will have become almost perfectly symmetrical. Barring major accidents, we then should remain level-headed for the rest of our lives.

How Permanent Are Birthmarks?

I t is rare for a baby to be born with a completely unblemished skin. If the surface of the newborn is examined carefully enough, it is nearly always possible to detect some small mark or discoloration. When first observed, this often distresses new parents, who fear they have discovered a lasting defect. However, the happy fact is that hardly any of these birthmarks are permanent, and the vast majority of them disappear in a very short space of time.

There are several different types of skin blemish:

1. *Pressure marks.* These are red patches caused by the crushing of the skin of the newborn during its difficult passage through the birth canal. They are no cause for concern and disappear within a few days after birth.

2. *Stork bites.* Also known as salmon patches or stork's beak marks, these are pinkish-red areas seen on the eyelids, above the nose, or on the back of the neck. They are common, occurring in about 30 percent of babies, and are quite harmless. They soon start to fade and are usually completely gone within a few months.

In traditional folklore they are said to be small signs of skin damage where the bill of the stork was gripping the baby's head, as it delivered the newborn to its mother. In reality they are little patches of enlarged capillary blood vessels. Because of this, they become more vivid whenever the baby indulges in an intense bout of crying.

3. *Spider marks.* These are small cobwebs or networks of dilated blood vessels that first show themselves a little while after delivery. They are found in nearly 50 percent of babies and invariably vanish within two years.

4. *Brown patches.* Sometimes called "café au lait" marks, these pale brown areas may become larger as the child grows, but rarely darken. They occur in about 20 percent of all babies.

5. *Blue marks.* These gray-blue patches look remarkably like bruises and have sometimes mistakenly led to accusations of baby-battering. They usually appear on the lower back region of dark-skinned babies. Nearly all black and Asian newborns display them, but they only occur on about 5 percent of white babies. They soon start to disappear and all have vanished within two to three years.

Blue marks are completely harmless, and it is unfortunate that they are often referred to as "Mongolian blue spots," giving the mistaken impression that they have something to do with Mongoloid babies. In reality they were given this name because they are so common among Mongolian or Oriental babies.

In some regions these blue marks have given rise to local superstitions. In parts of Japan, for example, they are said to have been made by Kami-Sama, the god of childbirth, and in Iraq they are welcomed as a sign of Allah's favor.

6. *Strawberry marks.* These begin as very small red spots and may go unnoticed at first. They soon start to enlarge and within a few months become raised, red lumps, causing considerable alarm. But then, without any treatment, they begin

to shrink, disappearing from the middle of the patch outward. This happens as the period of babyhood comes to a close, and during the second year they normally dwindle to nothing, leaving no scar. In some infants they may last a few years longer and in rare cases they may not vanish until as late as the tenth year. Beyond that, however, they are unknown.

7. *Port wine stains.* These are the really troublesome birthmarks because they are the ones that are permanent. Usually dark red, but sometimes purple, they have a sharply defined outline and are highly conspicuous. They may be found on any part of the body, but they seem to favor the head region. They are not a medical problem—purely a cosmetic one. In recent years laser treatment has been applied with a measure of success and, failing that, there are specialized forms of makeup designed to conceal them. Alternatively they can be worn with pride, as in the case of the last president of the Soviet Union.

The golden rule with all birthmarks is to leave them alone and totally ignore them. Either they will fade away of their own accord or, in the rare instances where they are permanent, there is little that can be done anyway. In one case in thousands they may require minor surgery, but this is always a last resort.

Why Do the Eyes of Babies Have Large Pupils?

N ot only are the baby's eyes bigger in relation to its body size than those of an adult, but its pupils are also generally larger. This is a special feature of being a baby and has a special significance. It makes the baby look more appealing to its parents and therefore increases the chances that it will be fondled and handled more lovingly.

To understand why large pupils are attractive to those who gaze into them it is necessary to examine the way they work. The pupil—the black spot in the center of the eye—opens and closes as it controls the amount of light entering the eye. In a dim light it is a large black disc, but in bright light it constricts to a pinprick. It operates much like the lens on a camera. But in addition to light intensity it also responds to emotional situations. When the eyes see something they like, the pupils expand just a little more than might be expected in relation to the amount of light falling on them at the time. And when they see something distasteful, they contract more than they should. This emotional reaction is completely involuntary. We do not know we are doing it and cannot control it, but others can see it happening and can register the changes. Again, however, they do this without being conscious of what is taking place.

If a man is shown two pictures of an attractive woman and the pictures are exactly the same except for the pupils, then he responds more strongly to the photograph where the woman has had her pupils artificially enlarged by an artist's pen. The logic of this is simple enough. If a female feels emotionally attracted toward a male companion, her pupils dilate. Since someone who is attracted to you is inevitably more appealing than someone who is unresponsive, it follows that enlarged pupils are themselves appealing. The male who sees a female with large black pupils likes her *because* she likes him. All this happens unconsciously, with feelings of emotional acceptance (or rejection) flashing back and forth between the pair as they stare deeply into one another's eyes.

Signals of mutual appeal make the couple want to be more intimate, closer together, and to touch and hold one another. This applies not only to young lovers but also to mothers and their babies. The mother is free to pick up the infant whenever she wishes to do so, but the baby cannot express itself physically with such facility. It wants to be held and fondled and to keep the mother near it, but does not have the muscular strength to initiate this intimacy. It needs help. One of the ways in which it gets this is by having larger pupils. They automatically transmit stronger signals of appeal all the time and make the baby more irresistible to its parents.

When the mother comes close to her baby, the infant likes what it sees so much that its already large pupils enlarge even more. The mother responds to this change, feeling a further increase in her emotional reaction—a welling up of love and attachment and an overpowering desire to hold and cuddle the baby. In this way the baby can control the mother.

It is important for the mother to be able to see these pupil signals clearly and this is made possible if the iris that surrounds the pupils is a pale color. Dark brown irises make the changes less conspicuous, so we might expect to see a large number of blue-eyed babies and that is precisely what we find. This is not so with dark-skinned babies, whose ancient origins lie in the sun-drenched tropical regions where heavy pigmentation takes precedence over everything. But it is the case with white (Caucasian) babies.

Interestingly, these "baby blues" nearly always change to brown or some other darker color as the child grows. The extra appeal is required when the infants are most desperately in need of parental protection. After that the irises can deepen, as the young human learns to look after itself. So it is that nearly all white babies have blue eyes, but nearly all white adults have darker eyes. The changeover takes place very gradually. By six months there will already be a slight "muddying" of the baby-blue irises, revealing to parents that their offspring will end up as brown-eyed adults. If the eyes remain completely clear and blue at this stage, then it almost certainly means that they will stay that way for life, enjoying a distinctive adulthood as blue-eyed adults.

How Soon Do the Baby's Teeth Appear?

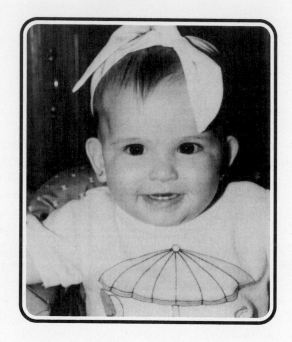

Some mothers are startled to discover that their newborn baby, from the moment it arrives in the world, has one of its milk teeth on display. They have a right to be startled, not because there is anything wrong with their baby, but because what they are witnessing is such a rare event. Only one in every 2,000 babies has an erupted tooth when it is born. For all the others there is the familiar toothless, gummy mouth that will stay that way for several months at least.

These premature teeth are called *natal teeth* and there is usually only one of them in a baby's mouth, although in even rarer cases there may be two. They are lower central incisors and they are nearly always poorly rooted in the gum, so that they move rather freely. This looseness means that they cause less trouble when sucking at the breast than might be imagined. They bend back in the gum with the pressure of the sucking actions and therefore do not hurt the sensitive breast.

Sometimes natal teeth are removed but this is hardly necessary and they are best left alone. In the course of time they will develop into normal milk teeth. If they are removed, however, there will be a gap in the infantile dentition, until the permanent teeth develop at about the age of six years.

In some cultures these natal teeth have been viewed with deep suspicion, as though they are a mark of evil. In parts of Africa, babies unfortunate enough to display a tooth at birth have routinely been killed to avoid the supposed evil that they herald. Needless to say, in every other respect a toothy newborn is just as normal as any other baby, although there is one quite extraordinary fact about them that cannot go unmentioned. Some of the world's most dominant men have displayed a tooth at birth. The list includes Julius Caesar, Hannibal, Louis XIV of France, Napoleon, Richelieu and, if we are to believe Shakespeare, Richard III of England. Bearing in mind the extreme rarity of the condition, this list is quite remarkable, but if it is any comfort to the parents concerned, there have also been many toothy babies who have shown no signs at all of wanting to rule the world. Today the nursery, tomorrow . . .

For the vast majority of babies, the first teeth do not show until about six months after birth. The exact time is very variable from infant to infant, and the "normal" range is usually given as between four and fourteen months. The most common range is between six and nine months. The lower central incisors are the first to appear, then the upper central incisors, then the lower lateral incisors, then the upper lateral incisors, but this sequence is by no means fixed.

Sometimes all the central incisors appear first, then all the lateral incisors. In other cases, all the lower incisors appear first and then all the upper incisors.

It usually takes about six months for all these biting teeth to erupt, and the typical one-year-old has most of them on display. Late developing one-year-olds, however, may have no teeth at all. It may be possible to tell the age of a gift-horse by looking at it in the mouth, but with human babies it is not so easy. In fact, checking the number of teeth present in a baby is one of the worst ways of assessing its age.

In the second year, after the baby phase is over, the cheek teeth or molars and the canines erupt and this is the stage when teething pains can cause infants to be unusually irritable and discomforted. But during the baby phase itself, the problems of gum pain are really quite slight.

The small milk teeth go under several names. The technical term for them is deciduous teeth, because like deciduous trees shedding their leaves they are shed from the mouth during childhood to be replaced by the larger permanent teeth. They are also called baby teeth or primary teeth. There are twenty of them and they start to form beneath the gums from a very early stage in the baby's development. They are already there in the six-week-old fetus, as tiny, growing teeth buds. Between the sixteenth and the twenty-fourth week of pregnancy, these buds start to calcify, as they prepare themselves to burst through and become functional.

There is a small difference between the sexes, where milk teeth are concerned. Girl babies' teeth come through their gums slightly before boys, but boys lose their milk teeth a little before girls do. Why girls should need their baby teeth for longer than boys remains a mystery.

How Strong Are Newborn Babies?

I n most ways newborn babies are physically weak, but in one unexpected way they are incredibly strong. From the day they are born they are capable of a powerful *grasp reflex* with their small fingers. Their grip is so strong that they are able to cling on to parental forefingers with their hands and hang from them in midair. For a baby that seems so vulnerable and helpless, it is an extraordinary gymnastic feat.

A word of caution is necessary here. The temptation to test this somehow inappropriate physical quality must be resisted unless the baby has a very soft bed to fall back on. The reason for this caution is that the newborn grasp reflex fades very quickly in some babies and in a few days may no longer be powerful enough to support the weight of the body. A successful hanging baby one day may be a falling baby the next.

The "lifespan" of the grasp reflex is curious. It can be demonstrated clinically in very premature babies and gets stronger and stronger as the fetus grows in the womb. It is at its strongest just after birth and that is when the hanging-by-its-hands ability can best be shown. At this stage the baby's body weight is not too great, but as it starts to grow bigger and bigger the power of even the strongest grasp becomes insufficient to support the infant's weight. Then the grasp reflex itself starts to become less obvious and with the baby getting steadily heavier and the grasp getting steadily weaker, the hand-clinging ability is progressively lost. In some babies it stays late and they can even be lifted up by it when they are two months old. Then there is a pause before the next major stage in child development arrives—the dawn of voluntary grasping, deliberately controlled by the baby as it explores the world around it.

This "advanced" grasping is not a refinement of the earlier, instinctive grasping, it is a new pattern that can only emerge when the earlier, more primitive response has waned. The grasp reflex of the newborn is quite automatic and is operated by the oldest part of the brain. Reflexes such as this and various other instinctive patterns of behavior that can be observed in the newborn human all start to fade away before the more complicated areas of the brain, the "new brain," begin to dominate the infant's behavior. The new grasping is variable and controllable. The infant can experiment with it and vary it. At about seven to eight months this involves the wonderful discovery that small objects can be gripped and then dropped or thrown away. For parents, picking up objects that have been "de-grasped" becomes an oft repeated chore, much to the delight of the playfully experimental infant.

Although this voluntary grasper has made great progress, in one way it has lost ground, however, for it is no longer capable of using this advanced grasp to support its own weight. That is a feat that will not reappear until the infant is about two years old. So, in this respect at least, the newborn is an Olympic champion compared with its one-year-old companion.

Many parents have puzzled at this remarkable newborn ability. What use can it be to a human baby? The answer is that it now has very little value indeed except to remind us of our very close evolutionary relationship with the monkeys and apes. Every newborn monkey and ape possesses a powerful grip right from birth, and young monkeys have even been seen grasping on to their mother's fur at the very moment of their births, before the whole of their bodies have emerged into the outside world. All maternal monkeys and apes have a thick coat of fur on to which their newborn can cling with ferocious intensity. So strong is their clasp that they remain securely fastened even as their mothers leap and swing through the trees, or scamper across the ground. It is this form of primate clasping that we are witnessing, in a relic form, in our own offspring. With other species it survives as a long-term reflex of great value. With us its uselessness allows it to fade very rapidly.

The way to demonstrate the grasp reflex is to press a forefinger gently but firmly into the palm of the hand of the newborn. It responds by clamping its fingers tightly around it. Interestingly, if the baby is allowed to suck while doing this, the grip becomes even tighter, as though the cling-and-feed reaction is asserting itself as a combined unit. Again this is an apelike quality.

If the back of the baby's hand, instead of the palm, is touched by the adult, the opposite effect is seen—the hand opens instead of clasping.

Baby monkeys and apes cling to their mothers with their feet as well as their hands. Amazingly, despite the major change in foot design that adapts us to walking bipedally, the human newborn still clearly shows a remnant of its ancestral foot-clinging. If the parent presses a forefinger against the sole of the foot (while not touching the rest of the foot), it is possible to see the small toes bend down in a valiant attempt at clasping the finger. The toes may not succeed, but in their attempt they reveal once again how close we really are to our primate cousins.

How Well
Can Babies See?

I t has been said that the vision of babies is poorly developed and inefficient, but this is far from being the case. The vision of the newborn is perfectly attuned to its special requirements. Evolution has equipped the human baby with precisely the kind of visual capacity that suits it best, given its physical condition.

Consider the facts: at birth, the pressure of passing through the narrow birth canal does the eyes no favors. Following delivery they may appear puffy, swollen, and reddened. Within a few days, however, this condition quickly improves, leaving the baby bright-eyed and beautiful, and staring intently at the world around it. When it gazes into the distance, everything is a blur. The eyes refuse to focus on far-away points. When trying to peer at long distances, they fail to work in unison and one may drift off out of line with the other. This lack of binocular control in distant vision is no cause for alarm. Parents fearing that their babies may grow up with a squint or with crossed eyes have no need for concern unless the condition persists for more than six weeks. This is the time it takes for the development of full binocular vision and for the strengthening of the eye muscles that move the eyes and coordinate the shifts in eye direction.

At close quarters the situation is very different. At distances of between 7 and 12 inches, the newborn is well equipped to focus its eyes and to concentrate them on the object in front of its face. It already has several distinct preferences. It responds more strongly to objects that move, as opposed to those that are completely static. It favors curved shapes over straight, geometric ones. It is sensitive to patterns. It likes big objects that are brightly lit.

What does this add up to? For the new baby it is the height of efficiency. Its blurred long-distance vision is a valuable anti-anxiety device. Since the infant is physically more or less helpless, there is no advantage in knowing what is happening far away from its body. Its blissful ignorance of the long-distance world leaves it snugly relaxed and contented. By contrast, it is crucially important that the baby should be sensitive to the presence of its total protector, its mother. The preference for large, curved, conspicuous, and slightly moving shapes close to the baby's face, and its ability to focus on such shapes, equips it perfectly to respond to the proximity of the maternal face.

So the baby sees what it needs to see and avoids the confusion of being able to see things that are of no importance to it in its first days. Nothing could be better designed. The old idea of babies being almost blind, and only capable of seeing the difference between light and dark, was hopelessly inaccurate. Anyone studying the babies of different species of animals would have been quick to see the stupidity of such an idea. Each species is well adapted at birth to see what it needs to see. A young antelope must have almost perfect adult vision from the moment it staggers on to its spindly legs. It must be ready to flee from its enemies almost immediately. A mouse, born in a dark underground nest, on the other hand, is better without any vision. Born blind, it will be more likely to stay still in the nest and not wander off in response to some patch of light. Its closed eyes protect it and it can rely on body smells to identify both its littermates and its mother.

The human animal falls between these two extremes of the antelope and the mouse. The baby is helpless enough not to have any interest in the larger scene, but from the very beginning it must start to make visual contact with its mother. This works two ways. It not only fixates the baby on its parent's face but also, by shared eye contact, helps to fixate the mother on her baby's face. The mutual gazing, at close quarters, starts to form a bond of attachment right from the first moment when the new mother cradles her infant in the crook of her arm. And it is no accident that the distance between her face and that of her snugly held baby is typically between 7 and 12 inches—the very distance at which the newborn is capable of focusing its eyes.

Recent careful studies of the behavior of babies just after birth have revealed that, as soon as they have recovered from the trauma of delivery, they will spend up to an hour staring intently at their mother's face, if given the chance, before falling asleep. Some hospitals routinely ignore the importance of this primary eye-to-eye contact. They favor the idea that both mother and baby "need a rest" after their exertions. This may appear reasonable on the surface, but if both parent and child are fit and healthy, it is far better for them to be in close eye contact during the first hour. In this way the deep bond of attachment between them can start to take root at this key moment.

During its earliest days, the baby responds positively to any face that it encounters in gentle, close proximity. It has yet to differentiate the mother from strangers. Gradually this changes, until there is joy at the mother's presence and panic when confronted with a close-up of the grinning face of an admiring stranger. It used to be thought that this switch to selectivity came at an age of three to four months, but recently this idea has been revised. As with other behavior, babies are now believed to be more advanced at an earlier phase of their young lives. Some authorities put parental recognition as early as three weeks, or even two. The explanation for this change of opinion is that there was a flaw in the original tests, with babies being shown silent, static faces, instead of moving, talking heads of the kind they experience in real life. Parents nearly always coo and chat to their offspring, and it is this combination of face and voice that the baby learns to recognize.

This special combination of vision and sound was studied by the simple method of showing babies silent faces of their mothers and of strangers. Then they were shown faces talking with the wrong voices. This was done by recording the maternal voices and those of the strangers and then getting mothers to mime to strange voices and strangers to mime to the mothers' voices. Finally, the mothers were shown to their babies with their own voices talking. At three weeks, babies failed to respond to any of the silent or "trick" faces, but immediately reacted to the magical combination of their own mother's face and voice.

Although discrimination is possible at this stage, the reaction to the stranger is still not very strong. It is more a case of positive interest in parent and no interest in stranger. There is not yet a strong negative reaction to strangers. That does not usually arrive until about halfway through the first year of life. Then, the cooperative, amenable babe-in-arms suddenly becomes a screaming dervish when handled or approached too closely by strange faces. The famous "stranger anxiety" reaction, that some parents find so embarrassing when it first erupts, makes its debut. By the age of nine months it becomes acute, as doctors know to their cost. Vision by this stage is becoming more organized and the growing baby is capable of seeing much more detail and of focusing at a whole variety of distances. Although perfect vision is not fully acquired until the child is four years old, by the end of the baby phase, at the age of one year, most of the adult qualities are present. Focusing is almost as good as that of adults and binocular control of the eyes is now fully operative. There will still be a little refinement in visual acuity, but effectively the one-year-old infant is visually adept.

How Well Can Babies Hear?

We now know that babies are capable of hearing sounds as early as three months *before* they are born. Thanks to modern technology we can study accurately the reactions babies make to sudden sounds while they are still snug inside the womb.

The earliest reactions were obtained from unborn babies in the twenty-fourth week of gestation. A sharp, loud noise produced a clear startle response. At this tender age the reaction did not always occur, but a month later, in the twenty-eighth week of gestation it was present in every case. So, during the last two or three months of womb-life, the growing baby is already a listening baby, hearing the rhythmic sounds of its mother's body and even reacting to noises from the outside world.

The sharper the sounds, the stronger the reaction. This is because noises are muffled, not just by the mother's body-wall, but also because the middle ear of the fetus is filled with amniotic fluid, which has the effect of damping down the incoming sounds and softening them. This condition persists until the fluid is absorbed from the middle ear, which does not occur until several days after the birth of the baby. Far from being a defect this may be a protective device, reducing the cacophony of sounds that bombard the baby immediately after its delivery. Even with the liquid present in the middle ear, the shock of emerging into the outside world, with the ears suddenly exposed to direct stimulation, must be considerable and the noises entering the newborn's ears must sound deafening. Without the liquid, they would probably be intolerable.

It has been argued that the reactions of the unborn baby to loud noises may be triggered, not by the sound itself, but by the startle response of the pregnant mother. If she is shocked by a sudden explosion, or say, the crash of a bottle smashing to the floor, then perhaps it is her sudden body-tensing that causes the movements of the baby in her womb? Tests were designed to investigate this and it was found that, even with the mother's ears covered so that she could not hear the sound, her unborn baby still responded vigorously with its own startle reaction. So the unborn really can hear what is going on in the outside world.

This observation led to the interesting question of whether a baby can hear the voice of its own mother before it is born, and become attached to her personally in this way. The idea may appear farfetched but it is not. Careful studies of the preferences and sensitivities of newborn babies have revealed that they not only prefer human voices to other sounds, but they also react more strongly to high-pitched female voices, than to the deeper tones of the masculine voice. This can only mean one of two things: either the baby has become attuned to its mother's voice through the wall of her womb, all through its final few months before birth, or alternatively there is a built-in, inborn preference for the maternal voice, established without learning as part of the natural maturation and development of the human infant. At present we have no idea which explanation is correct because every baby is automatically exposed to its mother's vocal tones during her pregnancy. Only by studying a group of exceptionally deep-voiced mothers-to-be could we arrive at an answer.

Either way, the baby arrives well equipped to tune in to the most important sound in its young world, namely the voice of its maternal protector. And this voice is terribly important to it. Mothers who coo and chatter to their newborn babies are doing them a great service. For there is a strong positive response to soft tones, just as there is pain and panic in response to loud and sharp noises. Curiously, without knowing quite why they do it, some adult males raise the pitch of their voices when talking to small babies. This may be an intuitive or even inborn paternal reaction, selected by evolution to help in the task of soothing the baby and keeping it content in its often alarming new world.

Special tests have proved that babies prefer human sounds to pure-tone sounds with the same pitch. In other words there is a definite bias in favor of human speech, even from birth. The speaking animal is already in the making. It has also been observed that, later on, when babies are in the phase of imitating sounds (usually toward the end of the first year of life), they are much more likely to copy human sounds than inanimate noises. They are, for instance, more likely to imitate words spoken by their parents than the ringing of the telephone. They are selectively channeled, in a quite amazing way, to respond much more easily to human than nonhuman sounds. This suggests a highly advanced auditory system well adjusted from birth as a language acquisition device.

To return to the newborn, we know that the baby is able to distinguish pitch and volume, and we know that different sounds can cause a number of changes: quietening of muscular actions, or a full startle response; blinking, crying, catching the breath, and even interrupting sucking at the breast. It is this last change that was used to test sound discrimination. It was found that if a musical note was sounded near the sucking baby, it would stop and turn its head. If the same note was then repeated several times, the baby lost interest in it and continued sucking. If a new sound was now made, say a bell or a buzzer, the baby would show interest once more. In this way it was possible to ascertain how many different types of sound were being distinguished from one another. The range was great and extremely impressive.

When older babies were tested for the reactions to sound of different frequencies it was found that they have an even wider range of hearing than adults. The baby can detect sounds from as low as sixteen cycles per second up to as high as 20,000 cycles per second. Although the lower register stays constant throughout life, from puberty onward there is a steady drop in sensitivity to the higher sounds. By the age of sixty years, the adult human is down to a mere 12,000 cycles per second. So, ironically, by the time you are old enough to be able to afford to buy an expensive hi-fi system, you are no longer capable of appreciating it. Certainly the baby would be better tuned in to its higher registers—if only it could appreciate the nuances of the great music.

There has been much argument about when a baby can first localize a sound and when it can first recognize its mother's voice. Earlier observers put these abilities rather late in the time scale. More recent studies have brought them more and more forward, as observational skills have been improved. Originally, turning the head in response to a sound was said to start at about three months. Now it is claimed that localizing sound begins as early as ten minutes after birth. It used to be said that several weeks had to pass before a baby could differentiate its own mother's voice from those of other females. Now it is claimed that this can be achieved even before the end of the first week.

The reason for these differences is that earlier observers were only impressed if the baby turned its head toward the source of the sound—a reaction that does not begin in earnest until the age of three months. However, closer examination reveals other tell-tale signs of reaction. The newborn baby may not turn its whole head, but it does turn its eyes. In one ingenious test, a baby could see its mother in front of it, seated in a sound-proof booth. There were stereo speakers on either side of the baby. These could be adjusted so that the mother's voice appeared to be coming, either from the left, or the right, or from the centrally positioned face. The newborn baby could easily tell the difference. If the mother's face and her voice seemed to be in different directions, the baby was upset. Only when the voice and the face both seemed to be coming from the front did it relax and look contented. This means that, not only is the newborn baby capable of telling where the sound is coming from, but it also demands that the sound and the visual image should come from the same place. So the mother is not just a face or a voice, but a combination of the two. Sound localization of this kind for the human newborn shows, once again, how well equipped the tiny human is even at birth.

Later on, the growing baby improves its skills. At three to four months of age, it turns both its head and its eyes toward a sound made about eighteen inches from one ear. At five months, it turns the head and then lowers it if the sound is located below the ear. At six months it turns the head and then raises it, if the sound is coming from above the ear. (This upward movement is a little more difficult than the downward one.) At seven months it turns the head toward the sound in a curving arc, improving the flow of the head movement. At eight months it achieves the most efficient kind of head turn, swinging it at any angle, directly toward the point of the sound. However, it is important to realize that these changes are not in the infant's hearing ability, but in its ability to respond to the sounds with visual attention. In other words, the human baby can hear well, *before* it can show us how well it is hearing.

As the baby phase draws to a close, words start to become more important. Babbling becomes organized. The infant is on the threshold of speech. Once again, experts differ regarding the time of onset of this phase. The earliest figures given are: twenty-eight weeks for responding specifically to its own name; thirty-six weeks for knowing the meaning of several words. Others think that these events develop a month or so later in each case. The differences may be due to improvements in observation, or to variations between groups of babies. It is always important to remember that the rates at which babies grow and develop, both physically and mentally, can be influenced to some extent by their environment. In the end however the gradual transformations all catch up with one another, as the remarkable sequence of human maturation moves relentlessly toward inevitable adulthood.

How Well
Can Babies Smell?

As adults our world is so dominated by visual signals that smells play only a minor role in ordinary daily affairs. We react strongly enough to the fragrance of expensive perfume, to the stench of rotting food, or to the smell of burning, but these are special moments. For most of the time we are hardly aware of odors in our environment. Blindfolded we would panic, but if our noses were plugged, we could continue with our everyday existence without any difficulty.

It is hard to know exactly how sensitive newborn babies are to the odors in their environment, but various tests have demonstrated that they are capable of responding to such substances as aniseed and acetic acid. Even in its earliest weeks, the baby's nose is therefore an active sense organ.

In addition to reacting to pungent chemicals, the infant has one highly sensitive odor response and that is to the smell of its mother's body. Careful observations have proved beyond doubt that the typical baby can easily distinguish between the smell of its own mother's breast and that of other females. It is possible to be certain of this because newborn babies soon develop the habit of turning their heads toward the maternal breast when it is brought near to them. This turning reaction can then be tested in response to cloth pads that have been placed on the breasts of the real mother, or some other mother. Babies consistently turned their heads more frequently toward breast pads of their own mothers and were far less interested in pads from other mothers, or clean, unused pads. In these tests odor was the only difference and no other factors were present to confuse the issue.

This ability to differentiate the smell of the nursing mother's breasts shows how well equipped the human baby is to protect itself from hunger. Even in the dark it is capable of turning toward the all-important source of infantile nourishment and revealing its interest in feeding to its maternal companion. In this respect, at least, it may be more sensitive and selective than an adult, although tests have recently shown that we are all rather more adept at using our noses than we have always imagined, especially where personal scents are involved.

The speed with which the newborn child learns the personal fragrance of its own mother is astonishing. Observations in cases where there is no artificial separation between the mother and her baby following delivery have revealed that after only forty-five hours the newborn can tell its own mother from other mothers purely by her body fragrance.

Even more surprising, perhaps, is the fact that mothers have the same ability in recognizing their own offspring. If a mother stays in close contact with her baby for the first half hour of its life, she will be able to identify it by smell alone if tested six hours later. Few mothers are aware that they possess this remarkable ability because in modern times they are never required to put it to the test. Its existence in our species suggests that there is indeed a powerful bonding process taking place during the first minutes following birth and once again this emphasizes the need for close intimacy during this phase, undisturbed and uninterrupted. This is a time, not only for seeing and touching and hearing the loved one, but also for mutual smelling, as the imprinting process between mother and baby is set in motion.

So strong is the newborn's sense of smell that even premature babies can discriminate with ease between different substances. It seems that, of all human senses, it is this one that is quickest to mature and the longest to persist into old age. Perhaps this is because it is the most ancient and primeval of all our senses.

If the smell of the mother's breast is so important to a baby, then what exactly is it that is producing the scent? Is it her milk, or secretions from the specialized skin glands that surround her nipple, or generalized secretions from her skin as a whole?

We know that when a litter of kittens is being suckled by the mother cat, each one sucks on its own personal nipple. It returns faithfully to its own nipple each time she arrives and lies down to offer her belly. There is no squabbling, each kitten going immediately to its own special place. This is done entirely by smell and it is clear that each of the cat's nipples has its own personal fragrance. This seemed so unlikely that some simple tests were carried out and it was established that the different nipple odors were the result of the previous sucking actions of the kittens themselves. In other words, the mother did not produce a variety of nipple scents, one per nipple, but the sucking actions of the kittens did leave behind their *own* personal scents and it was these that enabled them to relocate their own nipples.

It is entirely possible that this is what is happening with human babies and that it is the newborn infants that deposit the "personal" odor on their mother's breasts. They certainly do this with their favorite soft toys, teddy bears, and security blankets, as any parent will know when they insist on washing such objects, only to find that they have lost some of their appeal when they reappear, hygienic but odorless.

How Well Can Babies Taste?

Babies crave sweetness. Their sense of taste is well developed at birth and they do, in fact, have more taste buds than adults. Also, their taste buds are more widely distributed. In addition to those on the tongue, the palate, the back of the throat, and the tonsils, they uniquely also have a number of them on the insides of their cheeks. They are super-tasters, and yet all this taste anatomy is geared to just one kind of food—sweet mother's milk. All other tastes are intensely disliked.

Although we are aware, as adult gourmets, that there are thousands of subtle flavors in our food, we have to accept the fact that there are only four basic tastes, namely bitter, acid, sour, and sweet. If a baby is offered these four taste sensations, one at a time, it is disgusted by the first three, screwing up its face or trying to turn its head away, grimacing at the same time. If the offending taste is strong enough, it may cause angry crying.

The fourth taste has the opposite effect and stimulates active sucking. Furthermore, the stronger the sweetness, the longer the sucking will continue. If an adult's finger is dipped in a sugary solution and is placed in a baby's mouth, the tip of the finger is sucked and licked. If the finger is then taken out of the mouth, the infant tries to follow it with its head, leaving no doubt about the strength of its reaction. By contrast, a finger dipped in a salty solution is quickly rejected. After an initial investigation there is no sucking, the finger is pushed out of the mouth with the tongue, the baby's face grimaces and its head twists this way and that, trying to escape the noxious taste.

Clearly the human baby is elaborately equipped to reject strongly all but its natural, milky diet. As with other sensory equipment, this is not a blunted or vestigial system, just because it is specific and simple. It is a finely tuned, narrowed down taste responsiveness that is perfectly suited to the infantile condition. Babies hate such things as olives, mustard, pepper, beer, and coffee—and so they should. They are not gourmets. Where food is concerned, they are sucking, growing machines that would be at serious risk if they started experimenting with exotic flavors. Their numerous, undulled taste buds ensure that they are kept strictly to the milky way.

Although human adults do have a much wider interest in tastes and flavors, it is interesting that at times of stress they quickly revert to the infantile condition. Sweet things are reassuring. We find warm, sweet tea or coffee comforting when we are upset. If we are miserable we often develop a weakness for candy, chocolates, or sugary cakes—they take us back to the secure days of our sweet-obsessed infancy. (Sadly, without due care, they may also rot our teeth.)

How Do Babies React to a Loss of Balance?

If a newborn baby feels itself falling it reacts in a remarkable way. It responds exactly as though it were an infant ape, trying to cling on to its mother's fur. Unlike the ape, however, its actions are ineffectual and rather incomplete, but this hardly matters as human mothers no longer have any body fur to which their infants can cling for protection. The human newborn's attempt at clinging survives as a tiny reminder of its ancient ancestry.

What happens is this. When the baby feels itself falling, it detects its predicament not by sound or vision but by a change in balance monitored by the semicircular canals in its ears. In response, it reaches out as if to save itself. It flings its arms wide and opens its hands, spreading its fingers. If movements of its legs are not blocked, it flings these out too, curving them up as if seeking something around which it can clasp. The arms are then brought together as if making an embrace. After this there is a slow return to the ordinary relaxed posture. The baby may let out a cry at the same time, alerting the mother.

These actions do not necessarily make contact with the mother's body. They are automatic and usually result merely in the baby clasping at the air in front of it. The newborn has lost the full clinging response, but the relic gesture of it that remains is of some value to parents because it clearly hints that the infant is suddenly feeling unsafe and physically insecure. So it has become a useful visual signal.

It is also useful to doctors examining babies because it enables them to test for possible damage to limbs. The opening wide of the limbs is symmetrical in a healthy baby and by giving the newborn the sensation that it is falling, the doctor can check to make sure that both sides of the body are flung wide to the same degree. The test was devised in 1918 by a German doctor called Moro and the balancing movement is known today as the *Moro reflex*. His method was to place a baby on its back on a table and then suddenly jolt the table with his hand. Immediately the tiny newborn would fling out its arms and legs, clasping at the air. If this was done symmetrically, the baby passed its test.

This only worked if the baby's head was dead center as it lay on the table. If it was not in the midline, the test could not be carried out efficiently. A fascinating exception occurred if the baby happened to be holding something in one of its hands—say, a pencil. If its small fingers were clasped tightly around such an object, the arm on that side did not move when the baby felt its balance being disturbed. Only the other, empty-handed arm shot out to make a clasping movement. This is a clear proof that the Moro reflex is an attempt to cling on to something, for if the clinging posture of the hand is already present, it suppresses the movement of the arm. The reflex is so automatic that this happens even if the object is something as artificial as a pen.

Even more interesting is the observation that if the baby is clasping its own thumb within its curled fingers, this is still sufficient to cancel the flinging out of the arm. If both hands are thumb-clasped in this way, neither arm is flung wide. This demonstrates the comforting value of "holding your own thumbs." It clearly gives the sensation that you are hanging on to something that will protect you.

Doctors today use a slightly different technique to elicit the

Moro reflex. They hold the baby, faceup, with one hand supporting the body and one beneath the head. They then drop the hand that supports the head by a few inches. The baby, feeling its head starting to fall, rapidly makes the balancing action.

Anyone who has had the opportunity to carry a baby chimpanzee will have met this action many times. With the baby ape clinging to your coat, you sit down and relax. The infant ape relaxes with you, loosening its grip. The moment your body tenses or shifts, as if to rise, you feel the little arms and legs fling themselves instantly around you and the hands clasp your coat firmly once more. This is the Moro reflex in its full functional form.

With apes it is present for years, but with human infants it rapidly vanishes. It is present in all babies immediately after birth and at the age of six weeks it is still present in 97 percent of all babies. It then starts to diminish in intensity and has sometimes gone by the age of two months. Three to four months is the more usual time for it finally to disappear, although in exceptional cases it may survive to six months.

It is surprising how many authorities confuse this Moro reflex with the startle reflex. This is subtly different in detail and does not decline with the passing weeks. In fact it survives right into adulthood, becoming even more marked. Make a loud bang behind any unsuspecting adult and you will see it very clearly. The body automatically stiffens, the shoulders hunch, and the arms jerk up as if to protect the victim. But there is no wide-flung clasping action of the arms. They are much more bent at the elbow than in the Moro reflex, with the hands remaining more closed. This is a defensive response rather than a primeval fur-clinging, and the two should not be treated as a single reaction.

How Well Can Babies Control Their Temperatures?

N ot very well, is the short answer. When it comes to avoiding overheating and overcooling, babies are at a considerable disadvantage compared with adults. They need all the help they can get to achieve a comfortable balance.

If adults feel too hot, they can move away from the source of heat to a cooler spot. Babies cannot do this. If they feel themselves overheating, all they can do is to cry as noisily as possible. This may bring assistance, but it also, ironically, increases their internal heat production in a dramatic way. The intense physical effort of loud crying raises the body's metabolism and the unfortunate baby, if it is not rescued quickly enough, will get hotter than ever.

If adults feel too hot, they can remove some clothing. Babies will try to kick off their warm coverings if they overheat, but if they are tightly wrapped up, they may fail to do this. Again they may suffer in a way that adults simply do not have to face (unless they are soldiers on parade in full uniform during a summer heatwave).

Adults can also solve their problem by verbal communication, demanding that a window be opened or a fire turned off. Again, babies cannot yet make such specific requests. All they can do is to cry and scream. This indicates that they are unhappy, but does not tell the parents why. If it is supposed that the crying is caused by hunger, the giving of hot milk from breast or bottle will only serve to deliver a little more heat to the internal system. If adults take hot drinks they can use the liquid to service their sweat glands. Evaporation of the sweat from the skin helps to cool them. Not so, with the newborn baby. The sweat glands of babies are poorly developed and they lack this particular cooling mechanism. It is not until the infant has reached two years of age that it can sweat as efficiently as its parents.

As if this were not enough, newborn babies are well supplied with insulating layers of fat. Once more, this reduces heat loss and contributes to their difficulties when the temperature rises too high. Also their skin is thin and highly sensitive. Placed too near to the fire they may quickly develop red marks and patches.

Clearly, then, it is one of the basic duties of human parents to ensure that their babies do not suffer from overheating. They must also take care to avoid the opposite danger—overcooling. Babies are highly vulnerable to this as well. They cannot shiver efficiently—if at all, when they are very young, and the absence of this emergency reaction to extreme cold is a grave disadvantage. Also, unlike adults, they cannot put on extra clothes when they feel chilly. An overheated baby does have the chance of kicking itself free from its hot covering, but a cold one cannot manage to cover itself up. If they urinate and wet themselves, the evaporation of the liquid adds to the cooling process. If, as is the case with so many babies, they are bald, there will be considerable heat loss through the head skin, even when the rest of their bodies is covered up. If they are restless in the night, they can easily struggle loose from their bedclothes and this again can lead to added cooling.

There is another cooling hazard with young babies. When they are in a deep sleep their metabolism does not start to respond to a drop in room temperature at the point where it is needed. It fails to react until they are rousing themselves from sleep and are almost awake. A long sleep in a cold room is therefore a danger to a newborn baby.

When the baby is premature the situation is even worse. This is because it is during the final weeks of normal pregnancy—the weeks such babies have missed—that special layers of brown fat are laid down in the body. This fat is especially important in internal heat production and without it the premature baby can cool rapidly and dangerously if conditions are not right. This is why premature babies have to be kept in incubators at high temperatures. If they are to be comfortable, naked premature babies must be kept at just over 90°F (32°C), but then special care has to be taken to ensure that they do not overheat and thermostats have to be very accurate to prevent the temperature of the chamber from rising above 95°F (35°C).

Surveying all these various inefficiencies in temperature control, it would seem that the human baby has been rather poorly served by evolution in this respect. Why is the newborn not better equipped to face potentially damaging fluctuations in outside temperatures? The answer, almost certainly, is that mankind evolved in a gentle, warm climate, where temperature problems were not too severe for babies. Of the two hazards, overcooling is more risky than overheating, and this simply did not occur. If it was chilly at night, the primitive mother would hold the baby close to her warming body and sleep with it in this way, snug and secure. All she had to do during the day was to ensure that it was not exposed to direct sunlight that could damage its sensitive skin or overheat its vulnerable body. In a warm climate the problems were not then too acute, but when our species became so successful that it spread and spread, covering the whole globe, new dangers arose. In the colder climes babies were at serious risk from chilling and at this point heavy, warm clothing became a vital necessity. These climates were not natural for man, and our ancestors no doubt lost many of their newborn infants as the price they paid for their explorations to the north and south of the planet.

Today, with central heating and air-conditioning, babies are once again able to enjoy the comforts of more "natural" temperature levels. Because these "natural" temperatures are achieved by completely artificial means, new mothers have to take special care to provide the right levels. In temperate climates these are usually slightly higher than the mothers themselves might have chosen. This is because as adults they have adjusted to living in regions that are colder than "normal" for our species (thinking in terms of the million years we spent evolving in the warmer regions of the globe). Also influencing us is the fact that our bodies are cooler than those of our babies. The body temperature of human beings decreases slightly as we advance from babyhood to old age. So to feel comfortable babies need a room which is slightly warmer than the parents would have it themselves.

There is a scientific way to calculate the correct temperature for the room. This takes into account two factors: the neutral temperature for the baby and the effect of clothing wrapped around its body. The neutral temperature or, to give it its correct name, the "neutral thermal environment" is the level at which the baby can maintain its body temperature with the least effort. Like any animal, the newborn baby has to expend energy to keep up its body heat if its surroundings are cool. Heat is produced by the metabolic processes of the body and by muscular activity. If the baby increases its metabolism dramatically to keep warm it is in danger of depleting its body reserves rather rapidly, compared with an adult. It is also severely limited in what it can achieve with muscular activity. It does however have one additional protective mechanism—and one which is unique to the newborn baby—namely the large deposit of brown fat mentioned earlier. This store of fat, which is concentrated in the region of its back and neck, can liberate heat by a special chemical process and is of great value to the infant during its early days, should the environmental temperature be a little low.

These heating systems are given the lightest task when the temperature outside the body is at about 90°F (32°C), but it must be stressed that this is for a newborn baby that is completely naked. If the baby is wrapped in warm clothing, the room temperature can be much lower and yet still result in a high level inside the clothes. For instance, the temperature inside a baby's shawl was 89°F (32°C) when the thermometer outside it read only 77°F (25°C). It follows that a room kept close to this temperature will give the baby almost perfect "neutral" conditions. It can, of course, be a little cooler without any undue risk, and 75°F (24°C) is the one usually given as the recommended room temperature for clothed newborn babies. Earlier authorities put the figure lower, at about 70°F (21°C), but although babies can cope with this cooler room, the higher temperature is now preferred. In particular it is emphasized that when the infant is undressed for any reason extra warmth is essential, until it has been re-covered.

As the early days pass, the need for high temperatures gradually declines. Within a few weeks babies are able to improve their heat production and body temperature control. Now a steady room temperature of 68 to 70°F (20–21°C) is perfectly acceptable. Snugly wrapped babies thrive at such levels as they leave their early days behind them. Even now though, care has to be taken not to chill them when they are temporarily unclothed for changing or bathing.

To sum up, once they are a few weeks old, human babies can stand minor variations in environmental temperatures, but dramatic changes, especially those involving chilling, are dangerous. An unmonitored sharp drop, or sharp rise, in temperature has to be avoided. Rooms that become freezing cold at night when parents are slumbering, or unguarded moments when a baby is exposed to intense sunlight or "glasshouse" heating, are hazards against which the infant has little defense.

Why Do
Babies Cry?

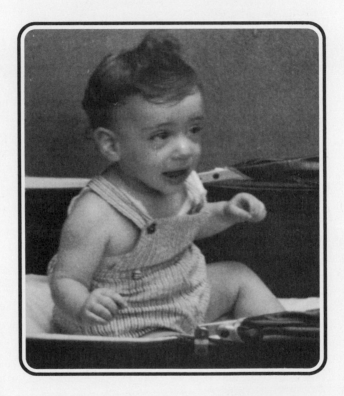

Crying is the baby's distress call and, in the absence of verbal communication, is its most important signaling system during the first twelve months of life. It is a nonspecific request for help that attracts the urgent attention of the parent, although it is not always immediately clear what the problem might be. It is an emergency device, the main function of which is to bring the parent close to the baby as rapidly as possible. Once there, the parent can simultaneously offer comfort and run a check to identify the cause of the reaction.

There are seven main causes of crying. They are pain, discomfort, hunger, loneliness, overstimulation, understimulation, and frustration.

If as adults we bang our heads or trap our fingers, we may yell and curse but we no longer resort to crying. The baby, however, is quick to cry with any sharp pain and there is a good reason for this. No baby can tell how badly it has hurt itself. It may have a small bruise or it may be more seriously injured and it cannot distinguish between the two. Its only protective course of action is to bawl its head off regardless of the precise nature of the pain. This brings the parent running and the nature of the damage can then be assessed, with appropriate action taken. It is extremely important that parents are never misled into thinking that crying is some form of "self-expression" or "letting off steam." It is always a plea for help and should be treated as such.

If a baby is wet or dirty, it may cry simply as a signal of discomfort. This is a milder form of distress and the discomfort cry lacks some of the intensity and sharpness of the pain cry.

If a baby is hungry, it may cry for food and will only stop when it is put to the breast or given the bottle. There is a difficulty here, though, if the infant has been crying for some time and has worked itself up to a high emotional pitch. In such a condition it cannot settle down to sucking calmly in a few seconds. It needs a little while to recover from the tension of crying. In cases like this, a bout of hugging, cuddling, and rocking may be necessary first to relieve the distressed condition.

Loneliness is a crucial factor in many instances of crying, especially in those cases where the more obvious causes are absent and the parent cannot at first understand what is wrong. If the baby feels isolated from its protectors, it may cry until it is once more in close physical contact with them. Being alone too much makes babies feel insecure and they will often cry incessantly until they are scooped up in parental arms. This repeated need for companionship may be inconvenient for many busy, modern parents, but the plain fact is that close proximity to its protectors is something that has been heavily programmed into human babies during the course of evolution and it is not an easy matter to condition them away from it.

Overstimulation from too much light or sound can upset a baby and make it cry. This is not ordinary pain, of the kind caused by sharp physical contact. It is a form of sensory pain, where the eyes or ears are suffering from too much sudden input. Babies cannot stand loud noises or intensely bright lights, and we sometimes forget this. On sunny days it is possible to see parents puzzled by their baby's crying, overlooking the fact that, although they themselves are wearing dark glasses against the glare, the baby is not protected in any way.

Understimulation becomes a problem with older babies, in the second six months of babyhood. Much crying during this stage is from boredom, and it is important that the baby's environment should, in some way or other, be provided with varying elements. If these elements are not the parents themselves, then changing shapes, colors, and patterns of some kind are needed to provide the necessary stimulation for the baby's sense organs.

Finally, frustration is a cause of crying among older babies who find their clumsiness or helplessness a barrier to fulfilling their ambitions. If they want to reach something but cannot do so, they may burst out into angry crying. If they attempt to achieve something and fail, they may start crying as a way of obtaining parental assistance in the small (but to them hugely important) task they have set themselves.

It used to be thought that the crying that occurs in these seven different situations was always the same, but we now know that mothers can distinguish between certain categories, even without special learning or prolonged experience. It would seem that mothers are programmed for this. In particular, pain crying stands out from the rest, its sharper tones producing a more intense reaction from the baby's protector. But predicting the nature of the problem from the precise quality of the sound is not always possible and sometimes, even after careful checking, the cause of the distress remains a mystery.

Crying can sometimes cause considerable consternation to the parent who is unable to isolate the specific reason for the distress. If pain, hunger, shock, discomfort, and other obvious causes have been eliminated one by one, but the baby continues to produce heartrending screams, the parent is often driven into a similar condition of intense anguish. If nothing seems to stop the baby crying, the parent may become so tense that this adult tension itself starts to contribute to the baby's misery, making the situation even worse. A vicious circle then develops, with the parents suffering agonies as their babies continue to transmit signals of acute distress.

This problem is typical of cases where babies have come to feel insecure through too much isolation from the parent. Their insecurity can only be calmed by physical comforting and relaxed, close contact, but if when the contact arrives it is instead tense and nervous, it does nothing to rid the baby of its wretched condition.

The agitated parent, the irritated parent, and the impatient parent do not always realize how easy it is for them to transmit their mood to their babies via their body language. Babies are sensitive to sharp, jerky movements by parents and quickly interpret them as signals of insecurity. These signals only serve to confirm and amplify their distraught condition, and increase the crying instead of decreasing it. The problem for the agitated parent is how to create a mood of security and serenity. This is far from easy, but if it can be achieved, it can work wonders in an amazingly short time.

How Well Can
a Mother Recognize
the Crying of
Her Own Baby?

W hen the new baby in the house starts crying in the middle of the night, its mother is rapidly awoken by the noise. Even a deep-sleeping mother who is usually hard to arouse will start up at the sound and become immediately alert. Is she reacting simply to the sound of a baby in distress, or to the specific cry of her own baby? Can she identify her own baby purely by the sound it makes?

Most mothers, when asked this question, reply that they do not think they have this ability. Typically, there is only one new mother and baby in the house, so it is difficult to tell. It is a maternal capacity that is not put to the test in modern housing. In earlier, tribal days, however, when the human dwellings were less isolated from one another, it would have been normal for each mother to be able to hear the crying of several babies during the night. There would be a great advantage to these tribal mothers if they could single out their own offspring and react only to relevant crying. Otherwise, all the mothers would wake up every time just one of their newborn infants began to wail in the night. But *could* they do it, and are modern mothers wrong to assume that they lack this special ability?

Observers in hospitals were surprised to notice that mothers did, indeed, seem to react more strongly to their own infants during the night. The mothers themselves, when housed together in wards, claimed that some sort of personal recognition seemed to be occurring. They felt they were more disturbed when it was their own baby crying, and it was decided to put this to the test. Special recordings of the different babies were made and these were played to the sleeping mothers to see how many of them awoke with a start and how many slumbered on peacefully. The results were astonishing.

After only three nights, twenty-two of the twenty-three mothers tested were able to recognize *in their sleep* the crying of their own babies. They ignored the sounds of all other babies, even if these were wailing pitifully, and they slept blissfully through these recordings. The moment the sounds of their own babies were played, however, they were wide awake in seconds. Some women were able to achieve this extraordinary feat even sooner. After only forty-eight hours from the time of birth, twelve out of twenty-three mothers were able to identify their own babies' cries out of a selection of no fewer than thirty-one different babies.

So this remarkable human ability is confirmed. It is an ancient capacity, hidden inside every modern mother, even though with today's living conditions she may not need it.

Not only does she have this sensitivity, but it is so finely tuned that she responds differently to the different kinds of crying her baby can make. She is aware of these differences even when she has only just been aroused from deep sleep. Waking up in response to her own baby's personal tones she quickly identifies which type of crying she is hearing. If it is pain crying, her reaction is lightning fast—much quicker than with other kinds. With those, she listens a little first before deciding to get up and go to her baby.

If we feel rather smug that, as a species, we have the impressive ability to identify our own young, it is worth putting our feat into perspective. If we were king penguins instead of humans, we would face a much more difficult task, for every time a parent penguin returns to the breeding colony with a morsel of food, it has to locate its own young, by its sound, from a vast flock of literally hundreds, possibly thousands, of otherwise almost identical fluffy chicks, all standing hopefully waiting. If our own achievement is remarkable, theirs is staggering.

What Comforts a Baby?

If a baby needs comforting, the actions that are most effective are those that, in some sense, symbolically return it to the womb. There is nothing mysterious about this, nor is there any reason to think of such actions as somehow "defeatist." Offering soothing comfort to a miserable baby is not encouraging "weakness." It is not retarding the baby's development; it is simply a matter of helping the infant through a bad moment. The more secure a baby feels and the more it knows it can rely on parental comforting when it is in trouble, the more outgoing it will dare to be at other, less stressful times. Being strict or tough on a baby is totally inappropriate in relation to its stage of maturation. Intelligent discipline can be applied to older children, but babies are too young for such treatment.

Inside the mother's womb the baby is hugged by the body that surrounds it. The flesh embrace is snug and warm. There is gentle movement when the mother walks and the muffled noise of her heartbeat. These are all elements that can be used after the birth of the baby, to offer a reminder of its lost uterine bliss. The embrace of its mother's arms, the wrapping in soft warm clothing, the quiet murmuring of its mother's voice, the rhythmic rocking of her body—these are all capable of providing comforting sensations. They may only rekindle one small aspect of the total security of the womb, but that is often enough to calm a stressed baby or to quiet a frantic one.

Each mother discovers for herself, sometimes intuitively, sometimes by trial and error, a pattern of comforting actions that work well for her particular infant. In one, it is enough to hug her baby to her chest and coo softly into its ear. In another, pacing up and down while gently rocking the baby to and fro is the solution. In all cases, the actions that are most efficient at calming and quietening are those that are performed smoothly, gently, and rhythmically. This is difficult if the mother herself is tense. Tension and stress make the adult body stiff and its actions tight and jerky. The voice becomes shrill, the movements erratic, and all these signals of uncalm are unavoidably transmitted to the baby held in the mother's arms. Sometimes a baby can be calmed and comforted simply by handing it to someone whose body is relaxed and whose movements—although superficially identical (the same embracing, rocking, and holding)—have a less intense, more docile quality. This is upsetting for an agitated new mother, who sees her baby calm down the moment it is passed to someone else to hold. But the message is clear—she must first calm herself if she is to calm her baby. Babies may not be able to talk, but they are remarkably sensitive at reading body language through touch.

In tribal societies, babies were held and carried a great deal of the time. In modern societies we tend to leave babies alone. We put them into cots, we place them in nurseries, we settle them into strollers, and we expect them to pass the time cheerfully and without too much fuss. But this can be extremely boring for babies and the loss of physical contact with their mothers feels strangely unnatural to them. They want to be with her, close to her, cuddled by her, patted and stroked by her, and carried around by her as much as possible. That way they feel far less threatened by the daunting new world into which they have been precipitated. And they do their best to let their mothers know this.

Some parents have reverted to the ancient custom of carrying their babies around with them by the use of "frontpacks"—little slings that support the baby on the adult chest and allow it to remain there, awake or asleep, as they walk about. The body rhythms these fortunate babies experience are primitively reassuring. Such infants are then more able to act in a bold, exploratory way, when the moment arises. They have been "security-sated" and far from weakening them, this strengthens them and makes them ready for new and novel encounters.

Babies that, for whatever reason, have to be left alone more than they would like, can be provided with substitutes for maternal contact. Little chimpanzees that have been abandoned by their mothers and must live in cages with no maternal body to which they can cling are often comforted by the provision of a "rag mother" that they can cling to. Many human children who, because of the parental regime, are feeling slightly starved of physical closeness, enjoy similar "rag mother" objects.

The other traditional comforters are the specially made "artificial nipples" that babies are often given to suck. These, by their oral contact, provide the infants with the sensation of being breast-fed, even in the absence of the real mother. This is enough, apparently, to give them the feeling that they are close to the mother's protective body. There have been many arguments as to whether such objects are to be welcomed, or whether they are to be shunned. In the end it all boils down to the question of whether the baby is miserable or contented. If it can be made contented by primary maternal contacts, then security blankets and pacifiers will not be needed. But if, for whatever social or family reasons, it is impossible for the modern mother to give her baby as much physical comforting as it demands, then the use of these various substitutes is clearly better than enduring a discomforted and wretched baby. The most important aspect of keeping a baby "comfortable" is to ensure that it is sufficiently calm and relaxed to be able to explore its new world from a secure base. The comforted baby is the exploratory baby.

Why Do Babies Weep?

Newborn babies cry but they do not weep. Crying is the production of a loud distress call, while weeping is the production of highly visible tears trickling down the face. It is a visual display that stimulates the parent to dry the baby's cheeks and to comfort it.

A study of 1,250 babies revealed that only 13 percent of them had been able to weep within the first five days of life. The majority take about three weeks and a few do not weep until they are four or even five months old. Crying is clearly a more primary response than weeping.

The most curious feature of weeping is that human beings are the only land mammals (with the single exception of the elephants) that shed copious tears during moments of emotional crisis. The eyes of young chimpanzees glisten when they scream with rage or fear, but there are no streaks of tears marking their hairy cheeks. With a copiously weeping human being, the tears flood the face and pour down the naked cheeks. Even in an unemotional year we produce eight pints of tears, and in a year of agony and conflict, with repeated prolonged bouts of uncontrollable weeping, the quantity produced is much, much higher. Weeping of this kind is a remarkable human reaction, and it is strange that it has been so little studied.

There are two questions that need to be answered: Why do human babies weep, and why do the babies of other land mammals not weep?

Ordinary tears, produced by lachrymal glands just above the eyes, are used to lubricate the surface of the eyes and to cleanse them. Blinking the eyes moves the tears and spreads them over the cornea. Old tears are removed down tear ducts in the corners of the eyes and replaced regularly by new ones from above. Under usual conditions the production and removal of tears is in balance, and there is just enough liquid to keep the corneal surfaces moist. If we have dust blown into our eyes, the tear production is stepped up and we may start to weep a little as the tear glands attempt to wash away the dirt. When we become emotionally disturbed, we also produce an excess of tears, but now the quantity is dramatic. The tears spill over the bottom line of the eyes. The tear ducts cannot cope with this volume of liquid and it must "leak" on to the cheeks and down the face.

Research into the chemistry of tears has unearthed two interesting facts. First, they contain a bactericidal enzyme called lysozyme that is vital in reducing eye infections. Without this enzyme, the eyes would be highly vulnerable to all kinds of diseases. However, there is enough of this in ordinary, day-by-day tears to guard the precious corneal surface. Weeping is not needed for this routine task. Second, the tears produced in large quantities during emotional incidents are chemically different from ordinary day-by-day tears. It appears that, when we become emotionally tense and agitated, the sudden increase in stress chemicals in our systems creates an unwanted surplus. If our agony leads to intense physical action, such as fighting or fleeing, then the stress chemicals are used up. However, if our agony creates a state of conflict that excites us intensely but immobilizes us, there is a surplus of stress chemicals circulating in our bodies, and copious weeping is a way of washing them away and allowing us to regain a more acceptable level.

The essential feature of typical emotional conflicts is that we are driven to do two contradictory things at once and this makes it impossible for us to obey either of the two impulses. We stay impotently where we are, literally or metaphorically tearing our hair out and suffering acute mental pain. If at this point we burst into tears, we are able to rid ourselves of some of the stress chemicals that have welled up inside us, and it is this special function that some authorities believe explains the curious phenomenon of weeping. Certainly the tears produced when we have dust in our eyes are quite different chemically from those that appear when we are emotionally upset. In the former case the stress chemicals are markedly absent.

The problem with this theory is that infant chimpanzees have just as much need to rid themselves of stress chemicals by weeping as do human babies. Yet they do not weep. The only way to defend the stress theory against this type of criticism is to suggest that perhaps human babies have more to cry about than chimpanzee babies. Bearing in mind how helpless they are when compared with the agile, fur-clinging ape infants, this is not so farfetched.

There is a second possible explanation of why human babies weep and that is simply that they do it as a visual display. Apes have hairy cheeks that would mop up and obscure the tears, while the naked faces of human babies are ideally suited to show off glistening streams of liquid pouring down from the rims of the eyes. It is almost as if the babies set out to "dirty" themselves, thereby eliciting a strong maternal urge to dry the tears and clean the skin. Human mothers do have a powerful, inborn desire to keep their babies clean and the streaming tears will inevitably bring out of them a caring, comforting response, in which they tenderly wipe and dry the small faces. Provoking this reaction automatically brings the mothers into close loving contact with their babies, which may be precisely what they want at the moment when their emotional upset streaks their cheeks with floods of tears. Of course, this and the previous explanation are not in opposition to one another— they may both be operating, giving the act of weeping a double value to the distressed baby.

What Makes a Baby Smile?

Nothing is more appealing about a baby than its smiling face. The first time a tiny infant's mouth opens into a broad smile is a memorable moment for any parent. But when precisely does this happen and what makes it happen?

There are conflicting ideas about the timing of the first smile and this is because there is a fleeting pre-smile to be seen long before the full, true smile occurs. There are, in fact, three distinct stages in infantile smiling. First, there is the pre-smile or *reflex smile*. Second there is the unselective or *general smile*. And third there is the selective or *specific smile*. What makes the baby smile differs in the three cases.

The *reflex smile* has been observed—by unusually attentive baby-watchers—as early as three days after birth. It continues, on and off, for the rest of the first month of life. Fleeting and poorly formed, it is barely recognizable as a true smile, but it certainly seems to be the precursor of the big grin that comes later. The most common causes are the sound of a high-pitched voice (nearly always the mother's), tickling of the baby, and gas after feeding. In the case of gas it may be accidental, but not when it is given in response to a voice or to tickling. There it seems to appear as a form of "surprise reaction"—a mild startle response. The baby does not jump, as in a full startle, but gives a "hint of startlement" via the smile. This fits in well with what we know about the origin of the smile. Like all facial expressions involving the pulling back of the mouth corners, it has an element of fear in it, albeit a very mild fear. And the turning up of the mouth corners as they are drawn back makes it into something quite different and special. Unlike crying, which humans share with apes and monkeys, smiling is unique to our species. It has become the friendly greeting signal of human beings the world over, and yet in its origins it is very slightly apprehensive. The fact that one of its earliest triggers is physical tickling confirms this. Tickling is fun, but there is the lurking worry that it might go too far. Is this sensation going to be too much? And the smile results.

The *general smile* arrives at about four weeks of age. Now the expression has matured and is a proper greeting smile. Each smile lasts longer, is broader, and is accompanied by expressive, twinkling eyes. The whole face smiles up at the delighted parent. The voice of the parent is still a trigger for this fully formed type of smiling, but now the more common stimulus is the appearance of the adult face, close to the baby's face. Parents often think that, at this stage, their baby is smiling specifically at them, but the chances are that it will give the same response to any adult human face that is brought close. This is the nonspecific phase of smiling. The reaction has matured and developed, but the baby has yet to sort out the appropriate stimuli. That must await the third phase.

Specific smiling comes much later. It can arrive any time between four and seven months, but is most likely to appear between five and six months. Like general smiling, it is fully formed and delivered to the onlooker with gleeful expressiveness. Simply by looking at the face of the baby it is hard to tell these two types of smiling apart. The difference is in where the smiles are directed. Anyone can receive a general smile, but only close contacts—individuals who are well known to the baby—will be honored by the specific smile. Strangers, who a few weeks earlier, were able to peer closely at the baby and be rewarded for their interest with a big grin, are now upset to discover that a similar tactic causes crying. The baby has at last learned its parents' faces and differentiates them from those of all other people. Smiling is now a highly personal greeting, and this makes it even more special for the mother and father. They belong to an exclusive club where strangers are no longer welcome.

There is, of course, a fourth stage of smiling—the sophisticated smile of the adult, but that does not really concern us here. Suffice it to say that, with adulthood, the more general smile returns—the official smile we give when we know we are supposed to like someone, regardless of our true feelings. When, as adults, we smile at strangers, we do so in a deliberate way, for social reasons, and we then use the smile as a formal greeting—a human appeasement ceremony that says "I am not aggressive, I am friendly." But such refinements are foreign to the baby's world. The baby smiles if it knows you and likes you and, with a delightful lack of diplomacy, screws up its face and screams at strangers (no matter how important they may be). It is this uncontrollable honesty that makes the specific smile to the loved parents so immensely rewarding.

Some parents believe that their babies learn to smile from the smiles they offer them. Parents will spend a great deal of time in intimate face-to-face encounters involving mutual smiling and soft vocalizing. They are surprised to learn that their babies would have smiled anyway at the appropriate age, even if they had not bothered to do this. If they had always approached their babies stony-faced the infantile smiling would have appeared, on schedule, regardless. It is not a learned response, it is far too important to leave to chance. Rather, it is a deeply ingrained, inborn facial expression of our species and even babies that have been born blind and have never encountered a smile, will perform one when they reach the age of four weeks.

Does this mean that all that parental smiling and cooing was a waste of time? No, it certainly does not. It is important for the parents themselves, because it helps to bond them tighter to their baby. And it is important for the baby, because it is gradually learning to identify its parents *as* its parents, a process that culminates in the specific smile at five to six months of age. And thirdly, studies with the born-blind babies reveal that, although their smiling is indeed inborn, it is never developed. They smile less and as time goes on without the visual feedback from their parents, their smiling continues to decline as the weeks pass. The baby that receives a great deal of parental smiling and intimate attention, by contrast, smiles more and more and for longer and longer periods. For those lucky ones, the smile becomes the most valuable form of communication during the months before speech arrives. Even after speech, the human smile persists as a vital social signal that lasts a lifetime. But it is undoubtedly in babyhood that the smile is at its most important.

The reason that we have it and the apes and monkeys do not is quite simply because they have fur and we do not. We share crying and screaming with them. Such signals alert the parents, both human and simian, to the distress of their offspring. They rush to their aid. Once there, the ape or monkey baby flings its arm around the hairy body of its mother and clings on as tightly as possible. This clinging ensures that it remains close to its protective parent. The human infant, having attracted its parent with its crying, has no such ability. It cannot cling on strongly enough to ensure that the parent stays close to it. It needs something extra—something that will be so appealing to the parents that they will not be able to drag themselves away—and that something is the smiling face. An enchanting smile from a human baby can keep a loving parent as close as any tight fur-clinging. That is its primary function. So, to answer the original question "What makes a baby smile?"—it is the need to be so appealing that its parents will want to stay with it just that little bit longer . . .

What Makes
a Baby Laugh?

Babywatching brings some unexpected rewards. One bonus is that by studying the way infants behave we learn something new about our adult patterns of behavior. The subject of humor and laughter has puzzled many thinkers, and there have been many arguments about the true nature of what we find amusing. These debates could have been avoided simply by watching the way in which a baby performs its first laugh.

The great moment arrives somewhere in the fourth or fifth months of life. It occurs at just about the time when the baby is starting to recognize its own mother and to differentiate her from strangers. The mother does something and the baby chortles. The first laugh of its life breaks the silence. The mother is delighted and repeats the stimulus. The baby laughs again, its face lighting up as it beams at its mother's face. But what action has she performed to produce this response, and what can it tell us about adult laughter?

There are several possibilities. Sometimes the first laugh is given when the mother bounces the baby up and down on her knee; or when she creeps up on the baby, makes a funny face and goes "Boo!"; or when she pretends to drop the baby and then catches it again quickly and hugs it in her arms; or when she buries her face in the baby's chest, puffs out her cheeks, and makes blowing sounds; or when she hides and then suddenly jumps out in front of the baby; or when she claps her hands together loudly in front of the baby; or when she lifts the baby high in the air and swings it from side to side.

What do all these actions have in common? The answer is clear if one of them is performed too vigorously and the baby becomes scared. Then, in an instant, the joyous giggling gives way to bawling and crying. Hugged and cuddled, the infant quickly recovers its composure and may soon start laughing all over again if the game is resumed more cautiously. This shows that laughing and crying are very closely related, and the old saying that "I laughed until I cried" can also be applied to many a baby. In fact, laughing is a cross between full-blown crying and the soft gurgling sounds that are made by a happy, contented, relaxed baby.

If you listen to the "structure" of a laugh, you will hear that it is made up of segments—a rhythmically repeated series of short exhalations resembling a wail that has been chopped up into staccato bursts. It is as if the baby wants to cry but at the same time feels that a real cry is not called for. There is something startling about all the playful actions listed above, which the mother inflicts lovingly on her offspring. She begins a rough-and-tumble action and then stops short. Or she gives the baby a mild fright and then halts. When she does this she alarms the baby, but only for a split second. The infant senses the danger—that it is about to be hit, jumped at, pounced on, dropped, or hurt in some way—and its fear produces a noisy exhalation of breath. But even as it begins to make this wailing sound, something tells it that all is well, that this is not a true threat, only a playful one.

It knows the threat is harmless because (a) the action stops short, (b) it recognizes that the action is being performed by its mother who is by now known to be its protector and whose actions are therefore to be trusted, and (c) it notices that she is smiling as she performs the action and is therefore in a friendly mood despite her apparent roughness. All this adds up to one basic signal. The message the baby receives is: This action is a safe shock. It is going to startle you, but you are secure because it is your loved and trusted mother who is performing the actions.

Babies soon realize that laughing makes them feel good. The repeated discovery that the shock is safe, that the threat is not serious, is such a relief, time after time, that it brings with it a special kind of joy—the joy of establishing that a fear is unfounded. This, the babies teach us, is the whole basis, the very origin of adult humor. The comments of the professional comedian are basically frightening, but instead of scaring us they amuse us because we know, all along, that this man making the comments is not, after all, a policeman or a politician, but a clown or a comic. We read the contradictory signal with ease—the signal that says unsafe and safe at the same time.

This interpretation makes it clear why babies do not laugh until they can recognize their own mother. Only when they can do that are they capable of seeing that the action is frightening while its source is loving. As I have said elsewhere: It may be a wise child that knows its own father, but it is a laughing child that knows its own mother.

How Do Babies Suck?

Once it has breathed the outside air, the first important action the baby performs is to suck at the breast of its mother. Shortly after birth it is able to acquire the valuable "pre-milk" called colostrum, a yellowish liquid that is rich in proteins and also in antibodies that will protect the newborn from infections. This protection lasts for a period of three months, until the baby's own defenses become more active.

After about three days, its mother's breasts start to produce the true milk that will nourish and sustain it in the months ahead. This milk is twice as rich in fat and sugar as the early pre-milk and it is a complete food that enables the newborn to grow rapidly day by day.

The sucking actions that obtain these vital fluids are not entirely new to the baby. Careful examinations using modern technology have revealed that they often occur inside the womb. During the final weeks before birth, fetuses have been seen to suck their own hands. Sometimes they do this so intensely that they develop sucking blisters on the backs of their hands. Clearly the human infant is powerfully programmed from a very early stage to perform these crucial sucking actions, so vital to survival.

What exactly are these actions? We call them "sucking," but do they really involve suction of the kind we adults employ when taking a drink through a straw? A closer look at the baby's mouth when it is feeding at the breast reveals that the basic action is more one of squeezing than sucking. The nipple itself is not sucked on; it is simply the nozzle through which the milk is delivered. The baby's mouth takes hold of the areolar region of pigmented skin around the nipple and squeezes on this rhythmically with its jaws and its tongue. The pressure forces the milk through the nipple, which is inserted deep into the small mouth. This chomping action, combined with vigorous swallowing, has the same effect as adult sucking and the liquid intake is rapid. Occasionally it is so rapid and the breast so full of milk, that the feeding process becomes too productive and the baby gags on the excess of milk and has to spit some out.

Overanxious, inexperienced mothers sometimes have difficulty initiating the feeding sequence. They try to force the nipple into the baby's mouth without any preliminaries, and they are surprised when the infant rejects it. This is because they have left out the first step, which is rooting for the breast. This rooting action is triggered by the nipple, the breast, or even a gently stroking finger, coming into contact with the baby's cheek. The reflex reaction to being touched in this way is a turning of the head toward the stimulus and a pouting of the lips. If this is done by the mother before offering her nipple, the baby is, as it were, primed for feeding and readily takes the nipple in its mouth.

Once the newborn has started to suck at the breast, it usually closes its eyes, switching off visual signals and submerging itself totally in the tactile and taste rewards of feeding. It is as if, at this very early age, it cannot concentrate on two things at once. By the third month the baby does more looking when feeding, but achieves this by sucking in bursts and alternating these bursts with looking at the mother. Shortly after this, it feeds and looks at the same time, and during this and later phases of breast-feeding, the bond between mother and baby is repeatedly strengthened by this combination of food reward and close visual sharing.

Certain mothers, with very full, rounded breasts, find that their babies exhibit the response called "fighting at the breast." It sometimes looks as though they are fighting against feeding, when in reality they are fighting for air. They want to feed, but when they do so the roundedness of the breast blocks their nose and, with their mouth full of nipple, this leaves them no way to breathe. Such mothers have to take special care that the position of the baby's head in relation to the breast is adjusted to give them the maximum chance to breathe freely.

This inefficiency of the full, rounded breast seems odd, especially when we look at the way we have designed the teats on feeding bottles. Babies that are given bottles in place of breasts are not given breast-shaped bottles. Instead they are offered much longer thinner teats, of a kind rarely seen on any human mother. They find these elongated, artificial nipples much easier to chomp on than the real thing. Why then, if this design is so efficient, have human mothers not evolved these super-nipples themselves? An examination of monkey mothers reveals that they do have elongated nipples of this kind.

The answer seems to be that the human breast has two functions. It is partly concerned with milk production and milk delivery and partly with sexual signaling. It is composed of fatty tissue and glandular tissue. The fatty tissue gives it its rounded shape; the glandular tissue produces the milk. If there was only the glandular tissue, human females would be flat-chested when they were not caring for young babies. This is what happens with monkeys and apes. Their chests only become swollen when they are full of milk. But human females have swollen breasts from the end of adolescence until old age. This applies even if they never have children, and the rounded shape of their breasts acts, throughout their adult life, as a specific gender signal. It is because of this sexual function of the breasts that they are slightly imperfect as milk delivery organs. Their hemispherical shape reduces the ease with which the nipple can be taken into the baby's mouth to the point where it makes contact with the palate. In struggling to achieve this, the infant may press its face so tight against the curved surface of the breast that its nose sinks into the soft flesh and it starts to suffocate.

The problem is easily solved by experienced mothers who learn to press one of their fingers into the soft flesh to create a "breathing space" for their hungry infant. The fact that such a measure is necessary underlines the dual nature of the human female breast.

How Often Does
a Baby Feed?

In the past when a new mother asked how often she should feed her baby, the experts usually told her to follow a particular schedule. Some said the newborn should be fed every one and a half hours, others preferred every two hours, or every two and a half hours. As the weeks passed, this interval was gradually to be increased to every three hours and then every four hours. Next, the nighttime feeds were withdrawn, as the baby adapted to the adult pattern of sleeping through the night. In addition to being told about intervals, they were sometimes instructed not to give in to their baby's demands for feeding between the set times that had been laid down, even if the baby was crying for food. Some mothers were sufficiently in awe of the experts to follow this rigid pattern slavishly, despite the fact that it nearly broke their hearts to treat their infants in such a regimented, disciplined way.

That type of feeding, known as schedule feeding or routine feeding, was popular in the earlier part of the present century, but has lost ground in recent decades. More and more mothers have refused to accept its tyranny and have bravely allowed their natural maternal feelings to dominate their decisions. Instead of feeding at set times, they have taken the blindingly obvious step of feeding their babies when they are hungry. This, of course, is what primeval mothers were doing for thousands of years before experts arrived on the scene and began to impose their artificially systematized regimes. Primitive mothers—and this can still be seen in modern tribal societies—feed their babies whenever they want to be fed, day or night. The babies are in close contact with their mothers almost nonstop during their earliest weeks, and their feeding is a remarkably relaxed, casual affair in which clock-watching has no place.

This natural feeding method, known as demand feeding, unrestricted feeding, or unlimited feeding, sounds like a huge imposition for the modern mother, but its rewards are worth examining. If mothers keep their newborn babies with them, day and night, from the first day, and offer them the breast whenever they want it, the frequent, brief feedings that result have a beneficial effect on the maternal physiology. This is the way that the human breasts are meant to function and it makes breast-feeding easy. The repeated suckling prevents engorgement. This in turn prevents babies being flooded with milk as the overloaded breasts disgorge their milk. If feeding is carried out at less frequent, artificially timed moments, the milk supply may build up so much that babies vomit with over-imbibing.

Secondly, because the baby only feeds for as long as it feels like it, and because it has fed not so long ago, it is not unduly ravenous. If a baby is kept waiting for its meal, it may continue to suck at the breast when all the milk has gone. This causes damage to the breast and cracked nipples. It makes breast-feeding uncomfortable and leads mothers to think that their milk supply is deficient.

In other words, spaced out, scheduled feeding has the distorting effect of giving the baby too much milk in a rush and then not enough afterward. If the mother feeds many times a day, on demand, this has the effect of making the breasts produce more milk overall, but prevents the unnatural buildup that causes engorgement. There is a gentle, repeated flow that suits both mother and baby. The mother's breasts work at a natural rate and the baby feeds at a natural rate. Nothing could be simpler, providing the mother is prepared to offer the breast at much shorter and slightly irregular intervals.

A curious bonus of this method of feeding is that it also acts as a moderately effective contraceptive. If the breasts are giving milk at short intervals day and night, the activation of the maternal hormonal system suppresses ovulation to a large extent. Again, this is a natural phenomenon, which helps to space out babies in a primitive tribal context, reducing the parental demands put upon the mothers. If milk is offered in the unnaturally spaced-out system of the schedule feeding regime, the steady, nonstop activation of the maternal hormonal system is interrupted sufficiently for the cycle of ovulation and menstruation to start up again. This is why there has been disagreement about the contraceptive value of breast-feeding. The value is there, but only if the mother employs natural, unrestricted feeding methods.

If demand feeding is adopted as the natural solution to nourishing the newborn, it does not mean that the mother will be trapped in an almost nonstop suckling sequence for very long. As the days pass, the baby will begin to establish its own routine. It becomes "self-scheduling" and soon starts to create its own pattern of feeding, little by little increasing the gaps between feeds. At the same time, the mother's milk supply will match the new demands. Evolution has provided her with this ability and few women should experience any difficulty if this pattern is followed. The fact that so many claim to have been failures at breast-feeding is due, not to any inherent incapacity on their part, but to the fact that they have been asked to follow unnaturally regimented feeding sequences, instead of letting the baby lead them with its natural needs, starting to suck when it wants to and stopping when it wants to.

It was the Victorians who were largely to blame for the trend away from natural breast-feeding sequences. They haughtily decried women who were too ready to offer the breast, saying that they were acting "like cows," and insisting that it was "improper and pernicious" to breast-feed too often. This form of puritanism was then augmented by the later ideas, in the first half of the present century, that "giving in" to the baby's desires was a weakness and to be avoided at all costs. But it was not the tiny babies that were imposing a tyranny, it was the authors of those statements. Their influence lasted for decades, but finally lost ground, although not without a fight. Busy professionals (whether hospital staff or the mothers themselves) often prefer a strict routine where babies are concerned, to facilitate the organization of their lives. If their artificial feeding rate makes suckling difficult, they can easily turn to bottle-feeding. This is certainly simpler to organize as regards the milk supply, but the babies will not benefit from the special rewards of intimacy at the breast. It can be an efficient and viable alternative, if properly administered, but it can never be as satisfying, for either partner, as unrestricted, self-scheduling suckling.

Which Kind of Milk Is Best for the Baby?

Biologically speaking, it is ridiculous to ask such a question. Clearly milk produced in a human female breast is more appropriate for a human baby than milk produced in a cow's udder for a calf. But the question has to be asked because in recent years the majority of women in advanced countries have elected to bottle-feed their babies with nonhuman milk. Why should this be, and what are the pros and cons of breast versus bottle-feeding?

Starting with natural feeding from the mother's breast, a process that succeeded well enough for a million years before milk bottles appeared on the scene, what are its advantages? They are:

1. *Direct delivery.* There is no problem of hygiene or sterilization. In conditions of poverty, bottles may not be properly cleaned and the cow's milk used may not be fresh. Dirt and infections can intrude and cause illness. Cases of gastroenteritis are far more likely with bottle-feeding.

2. *Personal fragrance.* The baby that is breast-fed quickly learns the personal fragrance of its mother's breast and can identify her from it. Providing she does not make the

mistake of washing her breasts too frequently and too vigorously, the baby will, through its saliva, leave its own scent on her body and this will be one of the earliest channels of "bonding" between mother and child. This "scenting" could, in theory, happen on the bottle or nipple with bottle-fed babies, but hygiene demands that these be cleansed and sterilized more thoroughly, with the result that there will be no fragrance left there.

3. *Slimming for mother.* The action of breast-feeding the baby completes the reproductive cycle of the mother, a cycle that began with the fertilization of her egg. The physiological process of milk production helps the womb to return to its previous size and speeds up the mother's return to the slimmer, trimmer body state that she enjoyed before she became pregnant. With bottle-feeding this reversion is slower.

4. *Slimming for baby.* Babies fed at the mother's breast hardly ever suffer from obesity. Those fed by bottle are more likely to grow fat. Their overweight condition is due to the fact that bottles do not empty in the same way as breasts. When the hungry baby starts sucking the breast it is full of milk and the baby can gulp it down greedily. But then, as the baby becomes satiated, the breast matches this satiation with its own slowing down of milk delivery. This means that the baby's feeding sequence tapers off in a natural way. But with bottle-feeding there is a tendency for the baby to continue sucking even when it does not need any more nourishment, simply because it is so easy to extract the milk from the teat.

5. *Personal intimacy.* The mother and the baby are inevitably brought into closer personal contact by the act of breast-feeding. Their flesh-to-flesh contact gives the mother a deeper sense of attachment to her offspring, and the soft roundedness of the breast is more appealing in a tactile sense to the infant. Bottle-feeding can all too easily lack this close physical

contact but sensitive mothers can, with care, re-create it simply by holding the baby close to the breast while offering the bottle.

6. *Sensual reward.* Mothers who breast-feed successfully gain powerful sensual rewards from the process of suckling. These are totally absent in bottle-feeding. It is no accident that the mother's breasts give her pleasure in this way. Evolution has ensured this type of reward, just as it has made sex intensely pleasurable, as a way of improving the chances of the survival of the species.

7. *Provision of antibodies.* During the first few days after birth the mother's milk contains special antibodies that protect the newborn baby from infections until its own defense system is activated. Cow's milk cannot do this.

8. *Allergy avoidance.* Some babies develop allergies to constituents in cow's milk. Eczema is more common in bottle-fed babies.

9. *Reduced demand on kidneys.* Because it is more natural, mother's milk puts a lighter load on the baby's kidneys. They must work much harder when dealing with cow's milk.

10. *Diaper-rash avoidance.* Babies fed on mother's milk suffer far less from diaper rashes than those given cow's milk. This is because the cow's milk is less easily digestible and creates feces that are more likely to produce soreness of the skin.

11. *Correct nutritional balance.* The chemical balance of human breast milk is better than that of any other animal, as far as the human baby is concerned. The nature of the milk and the nature of the baby's needs have been fine-tuned to one another during the course of evolution and it is astonishing that milk that has been adjusted to the needs of a domestic calf should be as acceptable as it is. Everyone knows that human babies are sufficiently adaptable to survive on the alien cow's

milk, but just how different is it? Cow's milk has more protein and less sugar. Furthermore, the protein and sugar are not quite the same type. Cow's milk contains much more casein and human babies find this rather indigestible. It forms curds in the baby's stomach and discolors its feces. The fat in cow's milk is made up of bigger droplets which are less digestible. Also, human milk has more polyunsaturated fat than cow's milk. There are higher levels of sodium and phosphate in cow's milk. The vitamins in cow's milk are less suitable for human babies.

All of this means that cow's milk is far less valuable as a food to a human baby. Today, many improvements are made to bring it closer to human milk and "formula feeding," as it is called, helps to narrow the gap between the two. Clearly, this is adequate because millions of babies have been reared successfully on it. But since human milk remains superior, why is it not more popular? What are the advantages of bottle-feeding that cause it to be used so widely? They include:

1. *Modest procedure.* The use of a bottle to feed a baby is less embarrassing in a public place. Bottle-feeding can be done anywhere at any time. Breast-feeding, given the social inhibitions present in advanced cultures, requires greater privacy. The concealment of the female breast, even in its maternal mode, is a strong factor in Western society. It is hard to understand why anyone should be offended by a mother breast-feeding her baby on, say, a bus or a train, but it does happen, and mothers are sensitive to this. So bottle-feeding is in this social sense more efficient.

2. *Less demanding.* Bottle-feeding is less exhausting, less restrictive and makes no demands on the mother's health. If the mother is weak or unhealthy following the birth, the bottle is a much easier solution for her. It gives her body one less problem to face. If she is taking certain forms of medication, the drugs involved may be passed to her infant through her milk. If she is a drug addict on heroin or is using cannabis, these too may

be passed through her milk, as may excessive alcohol. If she cannot give up these substances while she is caring for her baby, then it is clearly better to bottle-feed.

3. *Less "animalistic."* Certain women find the idea of using their breasts to feed their babies somehow offensive. Some consider that it will spoil their beauty or damage their figures. Others simply have a neurotic fear of the whole process of breast-feeding. Because the great value of breast-feeding has been increasingly recognized in recent years, such women have been put under some pressure to ignore their misgivings, but this pressure may only serve to add further tension. It is important that a mother should feel happy and relaxed when feeding her baby. She will inevitably transmit these feelings to the infant and this will help the development of a contented, relaxed baby who has a good, bonding relationship with its mother. If she is breast-feeding against all her emotional feelings, the chances are that she will transmit the wrong body language signals to the baby. In such cases it is better to give in to bottle-feeding and ignore the pressures to breast-feed.

4. *More available.* For some women there is no choice. They have to use bottle-feeding for the simple reason that they cannot provide adequate supplies of breast milk. If this saddens them they should remember that millions of women have, by choice, successfully reared their babies by the bottle alone. Breast-feeding may be preferable in almost every way but it is by no means essential. And there is one special bonus. If they bottle-feed their babies, the infant's father can share the task, something that is completely denied the breast-feeding mother.

Finally, one misconception must be mentioned. Women who think of themselves as "flat-chested" sometimes feel defeated concerning breast-feeding, even before they have attempted it. They decide on bottle-feeding because they are sure they will be inadequate at milk production. They should not be so pessimistic. In reality, small-breasted women on average have a better milk supply than big-breasted women. This may be hard to believe, but it is true because what makes for a big breast is a more generous supply of fat, not a more generous supply of milk-producing cells. And the smaller-breasted woman will probably find that her breast is a better shape when it comes to introducing the nipple deep into the baby's mouth. The roundedness of the big breast can sometimes be a hindrance to nipple insertion, rather than a help.

How Were Babies Weaned Before There Was Baby Food?

W eaning is easy for the modern mother. She can buy ready-made baby food of a soft, smooth consistency, perfect for weaning the baby off milk and on to a more solid diet. Even without commercial baby food, she can create the desired purée of fruit, vegetable, or cereal by making stews, using sieves, or pressing the button on a mechanical blender. But how did our ancient ancestors manage to provide the gentle, softened food that babies need as the vital intermediate between milk and solids?

Luckily there are still enough tribal societies, lacking modern technology, to give us the answer. Students of human behavior visiting people such as the African Bushmen, the South American Yanomami, and other tribal groups in the Philippines, New Guinea, and tropical Asia, have repeatedly observed that one particular method is employed: the food-kiss. This is the ancient method of our species and there is evidence that until very recently it was still being employed in the more remote parts of Europe.

What takes place is that the mother fills her mouth with food, masticates it until it is almost a soup, and puts her lips against those of her baby. She then pushes her tongue into the baby's mouth. The infant responds by opening its lips and sucking. In this way the masticated food is passed from mother to child and the baby receives its first nonmilk food.

This kiss-feeding continues alongside ordinary breast-feeding, allowing the infant to become gradually accustomed to this new way of gaining nourishment. Little by little the breast milk fades in importance and the kiss-food gains greater significance. As this happens, the baby starts to take small lumps of more solid food, and eventually the weaning is complete.

In this respect, humans were, for a million years, similar in their weaning techniques to the great apes such as the chimpanzee, the gorilla, and the orangutan. And it is well known that many other animals, such as wild dogs and wolves, not to mention countless species of birds, employ a similar technique when feeding their growing young.

In some of the tribal peoples studied, it was noticed that distressed infants could be quickly calmed by an older brother or sister, or some other family member, pressing their lips to the baby's mouth, inserting the tongue and passing a little saliva across. This token food was comforting. It was a primitive act of giving and eventually developed into a greeting. This is also true of dogs. Anyone who has returned home to be greeted by an excited pet dog will have noticed that it leaps up and tries to lick the mouth of its owner. This canine greeting is often called "kissing" and quite correctly so, for that is precisely what it is—a stylized version of the canine food-kiss, borrowed from the time when wild cubs would leap up to lick the mouths of adults returning from the kill, with half-digested food in their bellies, ready for regurgitation.

In the same way, human kissing has developed from the primeval weaning actions of our own species. Whether employed as a greeting, or between lovers, it is used all over the world as a way of demonstrating love, deriving its affectionate qualities from its primary function of giving food to the human infant. From giving physical nourishment it has changed to giving emotional nourishment.

Among tribal people the food-kiss is usually seen with babies that are three to four months old and this is the age at which most modern mothers would start thinking about introducing their offspring to baby foods. It appears to be the natural age for weaning in our species. Nutritionists tell us that the weaning process should be well underway by the time the baby is six months old, because by that age its mother's milk (or bottled milk) is not able to provide sufficient iron. Without other foods at this stage there are dangers of serious food deficiencies. This does not mean, however, that breast- or bottle-feeding must stop. Far from it. The milk supply can continue happily right through to the end of the baby period, at age one year.

Most observers report that sudden shifts in diet are not advisable. The infant takes much better to a gradual replacement of the milk diet over a period of several months.

Some babies take to the cup and the spoon rapidly. Others detest the change and must be coaxed along at a much more gradual rate. The variations seem to have to do with how easily different babies can use their tongues. In sucking milk from a nipple or the teat of a bottle, all the infant has to do is swallow. But with the spoon-feeding of baby food, it is necessary for the baby to employ its tongue more actively to transfer the food to the throat. It is this that many babies resist at first, with the well-known messy-feeding face and purée-splattered clothing and furniture.

Because of these difficulties, it used to be said that babies should not be weaned until they were nine to twelve months old. That was the official verdict about fifty years ago, but as the decades have passed the accepted weaning age has become earlier and earlier. In extreme cases it has even been suggested that weaning could begin at the tender age of one month, but this is going too far. The baby's tongue is not ready for nonmilk feeding at that stage. It is now generally agreed that four months is the ideal starting point, with the process well established by six months and the baby feeding itself by nine to ten months.

Careful observation reveals that babies only start to bite properly at four months of age and only start to chew well at six months (even though this is usually no more than gumming the food). It is babywatching of this kind that tells us that we have, after many vicissitudes, arrived at the correct age for human weaning. We should always be led by the behavior of the baby, rather than by rigidly defined schedules.

Why Do Babies Burp?

A common problem for young babies is pain caused by gas after feeding. Mothers have come to expect this as a normal pattern of behavior and they carry out a regular burping ritual at the end of each breast-feeding or bottle-feeding session. It is thought of as quite natural, and susceptibility to painful gas is looked upon as an inevitable weakness of the human baby during the first half of its first year. To a biologist it seems odd that this weakness should exist. The baby is such a finely tuned piece of machinery that it appears unlikely. Could there be some other explanation?

It is worth pointing out that women in tribal societies do not have to face this problem. The burping ritual is apparently confined to the more affluent Western cultures. So perhaps these cultures are doing something wrong. Perhaps painful gas is not, after all, a natural pattern.

What causes it? The answer is the taking in of a great deal of air along with the milk. As the feeding session continues, the baby's stomach becomes distended with a mixture of air and milk and the baby, to feel comfortable, must expel the air. It finds this hard to do and the mother must help it by holding the baby's body to her chest, with its face looking over her shoulder. Held vertically in this way, having its back rubbed or patted, the baby at last manages an infantile belching. Mother and baby relax. The ritual is over and peaceful sleep can follow. But why do tribal babies not suffer in this way?

The answer must either lie with the air intake or with the way the air lies inside the stomach. The lips of a very young baby are not sufficiently muscular to be applied efficiently to the nipple of the breast or the teat of the bottle. They cannot clamp tightly enough around the milk-delivery tip to prevent air from being sucked in at the corners of the mouth. The sucking action itself is powerful and it is easy to see how it can draw air into the throat along with the liquid. By the age of six months the baby's lips are much stronger and air is no longer drawn in in large quantities. The burping problem ceases.

This explains how the air gets into the stomach, but it does not explain why tribal babies do not suffer from it. All babies have the same kind of lips, so all must take in large amounts of air during their first few months at the breast or bottle. The answer must lie in the stomach. Here we do find a difference between Western and tribal babies. The Western baby is usually held in a more horizontal posture when being fed. The tribal baby is held more vertically. The mixture of air and milk inside the stomach must have a chance to separate so that the air rises to the top and escapes with ease, in small spontaneous burps. If the baby is too horizontal this does not happen. The air is trapped and causes the painful gas. The burping ritual automatically makes the baby more vertical and it is this that solves the problem. The pat on the back may or may not help. Probably all that is needed is time for the air to rise above the milk, and almost any caress would do as well to occupy the seconds while this happens. With tribal babies held more vertically, the baby can resolve the problem for itself, without any special maternal assistance.

Evidence to support this idea comes from the fact that Western babies carried in body-slings rarely need burping.

There are several ways to reduce the amount of air taken in by the baby. Milk that flows too fast or too slowly is to be avoided. If it flows too fast, the baby gulps frantically to cope with the large amount and this encourages extra air to enter the stomach. If there is too little milk, the hungry baby sucks harder and harder, again drawing in an excess of air. With bottles, the hole in the teat should not be too large or too small. Old teats that tend to go flat also cause trouble. Wrongly tilted bottles, with the teat not at the lowest point also supply unwanted air.

In addition to the feeding methods used, there is the fact that prolonged crying draws in a great deal of air. Gas rarely causes crying, but crying nearly always causes gas. Babies that want a little extra holding or cuddling and who cry for attention may give themselves gas in this way. Mothers who think that it is the pain caused by the gas that is creating the crying are confusing cause and effect.

A final point: if a baby is being laid down on its side following a feed, it is far better to place it on its right side than its left. Because of the design of the baby's stomach, this simple measure will reduce gas problems, allowing the trapped air to escape more easily.

How Do Babies
Indicate That They
Are Fully Fed?

When a baby has had enough food, whether it is being
offered by breast, bottle, or spoon, it reacts in two characteristic ways. One is to push the food, the nipple, the teat, or the
spoon out of the mouth with its tongue. The other is to twist its
head away from the food source. These two actions are obvious
enough signals to the parent, and would be of little special interest

were it not for the fact that they provide the origins for later, adult signals. Sticking out the tongue and turning the head both occur as important human rejection signals in many social contexts. The simple, infantile acts live on as elements in the adult communication system of body language.

"Sticking out the tongue" is widely used as a rude gesture. It is accepted as insulting without any conscious analysis of why it should be so. The truth, of course, is that we intuitively recognize it as a rejection of the object at which the tongue protrusion is directed, namely us. We know, even if only unconsciously, that we are being treated like unwanted food.

"Sticking out the tongue" also occurs in a completely different context when people are concentrating hard. Here, those performing the tongue protrusion are not even aware of the action, but cannot help doing it as they fixate themselves on their task. Children act in this way when they are playing with a special toy and do not want to be interrupted. Adults do it when threading a needle, making a sketch, or performing some intricate mechanical procedure. In all these cases the tongue is behaving just as it did when, in infancy, it rejected an insistent parent offering food. The message now, as then, is the same, namely: "please leave me in peace."

The alternative form of food rejection—twisting away the head—has also given rise to an adult signal, the almost universal head shake that means "no." When the baby twists its head away it nearly always does so by turning it sharply sideways. If that does not work (perhaps because the eager parent follows it with the teat or spoon) the infant then turns it sharply back in the opposite direction. In making these quick left and right turns of the head the baby is effectively shaking its head from side to side as it indicates "no, no, no." Since the baby has no words to express its feelings at this point it must rely on this simple body language gesture to convey its change of mood, and parents soon learn to respect this signal. It is easy to see how, from this early beginning, the adult head shake has developed as an international negative sign.

In certain parts of the world, especially Greece, there is a different head sign for "no." The Greek No, as it is called, consists of tossing the head up and back. This is far less widespread than the head shake, but it appears to have the same origin. Although babies are most likely to turn their heads laterally when rejecting food, they may also turn them up and back under certain circumstances. The one direction they do not turn them is down, because this would not be efficient in escaping the breast if the baby's face was pressed tight against it. And it is no accident that it is the downward movement of the adult human head—the head nod—that has developed as the widespread body language signal for "yes."

How Long Do Babies Sleep?

When an overnight guest is asked if he slept well, the joke response is to say: "I slept like a baby," which pleases the host, and then to add, "I woke up screaming every ten minutes."

Both statements are valid because babies do sleep far more than adults, hence "sleeping like a baby" means sleeping a long time, but they also interrupt their sleeping far more frequently than adults. The newborn sleeps more than twice as much as an adult human being, but instead of one unbroken nightly session, it dozes in short bursts throughout both the night and the day.

To be more precise, the average baby sleeps 16.6 hours out of every 24 during the first week after birth. Earlier reports put the figure much higher—at about 22 hours, but when careful studies were carried out it was found that this was exceptional rather than average. A detailed investigation of seventy-five newborn babies showed that there was considerable variation from child to child, from as little as 10.5 hours per 24 in some cases to as much as 23 in others, but with the 16.6 figure emerging as the typical sleep pattern.

By the time the baby is about a month old, its total sleeping time has shortened slightly to 14.8 hours. This continues to decline gradually, reaching an average of 13.9 hours at the age of six months. When babyhood ends at the age of one year, the infant is still enjoying a daily slumber of about 13 hours. (This only shrinks to 12 hours at five years, but is down to 9 hours at age thirteen, before being reduced to the adult average of 7½ hours.)

The slow reduction in sleepiness is not spread out equally during the night and day. It is the daytime sleeping that shows the faster decline. At birth, babies sleep almost as much in the glare of daylight as they do in the dark night hours. Careful observations have revealed that by the third week of life the typical baby slumbers for 54 percent of the daylight hours, compared with 71 percent of the nighttime hours. By the time the baby has reached its twenty-sixth week its daytime sleep has decreased to only 28 percent while its nighttime sleep has risen to 83 percent.

So, in place of the many short bursts of sleep throughout the day and night, there is a gradually emerging pattern of prolonged nighttime slumber combined with brief daytime naps. The ten hours of almost uninterrupted nighttime sleep is a great relief to the by now exhausted parents. The baby is becoming slowly adjusted to the human pattern of activity. Even its daytime naps start to merge until there is just one in the morning and one in the afternoon. This is the usual state of affairs at the end of the first year and, as babyhood ends, the morning nap also vanishes.

To sum up, a three-week-old baby should sleep about 8½ hours at night and 6½ hours during daylight. This may be split up into as many as eighteen short bursts of snoozing during the 24-hour period. The six-month-old baby should sleep about 10 hours at night and 3½ during the day, with the nighttime sleep being more or less in one long slumber, and with the daytime sleeping still split up into short bursts, or naps. But there is no cause for undue concern should one particular baby not conform to this pattern, as there is much variation from individual to individual.

Where Do Babies Sleep?

I n modern times, the most popular sleeping regime for the baby is to isolate it in a nursery where it is left to lie in its cot. The nursery room is often beautifully decorated and tastefully furnished. The cot is snug and warm and soft. But is this really what the human baby wants? Is it natural for it to be left alone in this way? A little objective observation soon gives us the answer, although it may not be the one we want to hear.

The fact is that nurseries are more attractive to mothers than they are to babies. Any human baby would far rather be in its mother's arms in a drab hovel than alone in the most expensive designer nursery. The proof of this lies in the frequency of the human distress call that occurs in the two contexts. Crying and screaming are calls for help. They are not manipulative attempts on the part of "evil infants" who are scheming and plotting to dominate their long-suffering parents, although such a suggestion has been put forward in all seriousness in the past. Of course, ludicrous comments of this kind would not have been provoked had there not been something amiss. What was wrong was that nursery babies, unnaturally isolated from their parents, were screaming in protest.

Parents either left them to cry until "the baby's will was broken," or they kept rushing to the nursery to comfort them. If they had enough compassion to make the repeated dashes to the cot, they were faced with the task of calming down the distraught infant and getting it back to sleep. All was then quiet for a while, until the baby reawoke and burst into tears of panic once more. From such a routine came exhaustion for both parents and baby, and a regime that ended up punishing everyone concerned. Little wonder that early experts began trying to help out with suggestions of a more severe approach to nighttime crying. It is unfortunate that they did not stop to watch babies and learn from them, instead of proposing solutions based on inappropriate training and discipline.

Babies kept with their mothers night and day do not display these prolonged bouts of screaming and crying. In tribal societies infants nearly always sleep with their mothers. They remain in close body contact as much as possible and this dramatically reduces their distress calls. In this respect, today's remaining tribal societies are following the pattern that was undoubtedly present from mankind's earliest primeval times. In those remote, primitive days, it would have been far too dangerous to leave babies isolated. As a way of ensuring that this did not happen, the human infant evolved a piercing and intensely energetic panic signal and produced it the moment it felt itself being separated from its all-protective parental figure. Unable to cling to its mother like a monkey and unable to run to her like a fawn, the helpless human baby had only its voice to save it. Mothers responded naturally to this signal and all was well. At night, the babies slept next to them, immediately available for loving attention.

This contact system meant that night feeds at the breast caused the minimum of disturbance. The mother's sleep might be interrupted, but in the simplest and calmest of ways. There was no anxious listening for noises from the nursery, no stumbling out of bed, no pacing up and down in the night to pacify the infant. She awoke in the morning rested and relaxed instead of frayed and exhausted.

If this system was so efficient, why was it abandoned? Several factors seem to have been at work. One was urbanization which, in earlier days, led to appallingly unhygienic conditions for the majority of city dwellers. In those unwashed days, adding a baby to the mess only increased the problem and this helped to promote the idea of keeping the sleeping baby away from its parents. Among industrial societies the baby has rarely been allowed to sleep with its parents, whereas a survey revealed that seventy-one out of ninety nonindustrial societies engaged in "co-sleeping" behavior.

A second factor was the rise of incredibly strict, disciplinarian educational theories. These were primarily concerned with older children, but the general philosophy of "spare the rod and spoil the child" was extended backward into babyhood by some authorities. Babies were left alone to cry to "make them strong and self-reliant." Interestingly, in the rare cases where tribal cultures behaved in this way, their social condition was one of warfare and strife. The warring tribes deliberately treated their babies and children in this disciplinarian manner in order to make them into more aggressive adults. And it worked.

In addition to the ideas that babies isolated in nursery cots would be better protected from infection and would learn from an early age to become independent, there was a third factor: the fear of smothering the infant if it shared the parental bed. The suggestion that parents might roll on top of their babies and suffocate them is an extraordinary one, when one thinks of our species spending its first million years without the "benefit" of separate nurseries. But there is a good reason why this idea came into being. Where the custom of tight swaddling, often on stiff cradle boards, was extended into the hours of darkness, the tiny babies could hardly move a muscle. If such babies were put close to their parents for sleeping, there was a slight risk that suffocation could occur because the baby could do little to protect itself. But an unswaddled baby is a different matter, quick to squirm, wriggle, and scream if in trouble. Activity of this kind would be quite enough to awaken any parent who was not heavily sedated by sleeping pills, drugs, or alcohol. In fact, healthy, normal parents are extremely sensitive to the close presence of their sleeping babies, even when they themselves are soundly slumbering. Their resting brains remain alert to any signals of infantile distress and they quickly make any necessary adjustments of position.

So, to sum up, the baby that sleeps with its parents has the advantage that its physical condition will be more closely monitored. If it is too hot or too cold, or is suffering any form of physical discomfort, its parents will know of these problems more quickly than if it is in a cot in a separate nursery room. Co-sleeping is therefore healthier. The baby also has the enormous advantage of feeling more secure and more loved which, in later life, will make it *more* independent, not less. It will be able to explore the world from the safety of its origins, instead of fearing the world because of its "broken will." It will be outgoing but less violent, creative rather than destructive.

Co-sleeping is probably important for the mother as well as the baby. It has been suggested that the well-known phenomenon of "postnatal depression" is due almost entirely to the feeling of anticlimax the mother experiences after the baby in her womb has been distanced from her by social custom, first in the hospital and then in the nursery. It is claimed that mothers who are allowed to keep their babies near to them in the ward and then in the home bedroom do not suffer from postnatal depression because the continued presence of their newborn makes them feel fulfilled. Their hormonal condition demands that they should indulge in a great deal of cuddling and closeness and without it they feel deprived and "worthless." If co-sleeping can rid new mothers of their frequent feelings of depression, then that is an important additional reason for dispensing with the traditional nursery, at least during the earliest months of babyhood.

Against all of this it must be added that, if the super-closeness of sleeping with the baby causes the parents distress, this distress will communicate itself to the baby and will counteract the benefits of close-contact sleeping. If the baby becomes an "intrusion" into the relationship between the mother and the father, then some sort of compromise has to be found, for the baby's sake as well as the parents'. For some couples the ideal compromise is to have the baby in a cot alongside their bed, rather than actually inside the bed. This gives the best of both worlds—mother/father intimacy and parent/baby intimacy. Simply reaching out a hand can lead to contact with the baby and a small movement can sweep it up into the mother's arms for comfort or feeding, without her having to leave the peace of the parental bed. The baby can be monitored minute by minute and yet, during its long periods of sleep, the parents can enjoy one another's intimate company in the way they did before the baby's arrival on the scene.

In many ways, this compromise is even closer to the primeval situation than the three-in-a-bed solution. The modern bed tends to throw individuals unusually close to one another, whereas the primeval sleeping arrangements, with individuals sleeping on some kind of bedding on the ground, would have been slightly less "clustering" in effect. But the exact position of the baby in relation to its parents is less vital than the fact that it is within reach of them at night. So long as the baby sleeps near the parents it can benefit from the possibility of immediate contact at any moment, and that is what makes it feel secure—the knowledge that its protectors are right there if needed. It is this that the isolated nursery baby is denied and that causes it to "exercise its lungs" in such a heartrending fashion on so many exasperating nocturnal occasions.

For mothers who have expressed their shame, in the past, for having given in to the "tyranny of their bawling babies," and scooped them up into their arms and carried them off to their beds, one can perhaps venture to suggest that the true shame should be for those who have instead given in to certain arrogant and misguided teachings and who have left their infants alone at night to cry themselves into a fitful, lonely, and unnaturally isolated sleep.

Do Babies Dream?

Yes, they do, but what they dream about will always remain a mystery. Perhaps in their dreams they float back into the warm embrace of the mother's womb and hear the sound of her breathing and her heartbeat, feeling once again the floating sensation as they did in the security of the amniotic fluid. Perhaps instead they dream of the latest impressions that have bombarded them from the startling new world into which they have been thrust—of bright colors and gentle sounds, of soft textures and strong arms holding them, of warm milk flowing down their throats and of rounded flesh pressed against their lips or their cheeks.

We can only guess at the subject matter of their dreams because, even as children, we have already forgotten our baby dreams and there is no way of recapturing them. Despite this we can be certain that dreaming is taking place because of the manner in which babies sleep. Like adults they have two kinds of sleep: inactive deep sleep and REM-sleep. REM stands for *rapid eye movement* and it only occurs when subjects are dreaming. The eyes can be seen to move about behind the closed lids, as though looking in different directions while following the events of the dreams. This is a lighter slumber than inactive sleep and babies do twice as much of it as adults. For adult humans only 25 percent of sleep is the REM type, but with babies it is 50 percent. Given that babies sleep twice as much as adults and that they have twice as much of the REM-type sleep, this must mean that, every twenty-four hours, they dream four times as much as any adult.

It has been suggested recently that dreaming is a way of making sleep so interesting that we keep on slumbering and get our full quota each night. If babies dream so much more than adults, this must mean that it is vitally important for them to remain bedded down for as long as possible, which is not so unreasonable considering how vulnerable they are. There is safety in sleep, and the physically helpless human baby needs all the security it can get.

Why Do Babies Like to Sleep with a Treasured Possession?

As babyhood draws to a close, between the ages of nine and twelve months, many infants develop a passionate attachment to a particular object. It may be a piece of cloth, a shawl, a scarf, a baby blanket, a duster, a soft toy, or some other article of bedding or clothing. Its essential qualities are its softness, its smell, and the fact that it has been a regular companion at times of going to sleep. Its softness makes it easy to cuddle and the popular name for these treasured possessions is "cuddlies." Because they help the infant to feel safe, they have also been called "security blankets." Their technical name is "transitional comfort objects." A more appropriate term would be "mother substitutes," because that is precisely what they are.

For the baby sleeping in a nursery, the moment when it feels in need of a little maternal comforting—and cannot obtain it—is when the mother is about to depart at bedtime. For some infants there is no suitable object available at this point, on to which they can transfer their affections as the real mother goes. Two-thirds of children grow up without any cuddly to comfort them at these times. The lucky ones do manage to find some piece of bedding, or other soft object, that is present in the cot and against which they can snuggle. They may cling to it, lay their cheek against its special texture, clasp it in their arms, suck it, wrap it around themselves, or keep it close to them in some special way that soon becomes a nightly ritual. These individuals are fortunate in that they can feel slightly more at ease when left alone, than those without such an attachment. For this reason, cuddlies do more good than harm. Indeed, they really do no harm at all, despite the comments of certain critics who think of them as somehow unnatural. It is not the cuddlies that are unnatural—it is the practice of leaving infants alone at bedtime.

In many cases, the attachment to a mother substitute does not begin until after the babyhood period is over. Frequently, it is the two-year-old, or three-year-old, who first becomes passionately attached to an object. A recent study of babies revealed that only 21 percent of the cuddlies appear during the babyhood phase—usually when the infant is approaching the age of twelve months. This is therefore more a phenomenon of the toddler phase than of babyhood.

There are two minor disadvantages with cuddlies. They can be rather unhygienic and they cause intense distress if they are lost or destroyed. Hygiene is a problem because part of their appeal is their special odor. If they are washed too thoroughly, they lose some of their charm, but occasionally this is inevitable. If they are mislaid, thrown away in disgust by someone who does not realize the object's importance, destroyed, or if they have simply disintegrated through repeated use, a crisis may occur. Should they be left behind when the family goes on holiday, there can be moments of acute anxiety. For many infants, these objects take on the importance of real people, and once they have entered the family scene they have to be treated with great respect. The simplest solution for dealing with both problems of hygiene and loss of object is to keep duplicates from a very early stage. No child will be fooled by these substitute-substitutes, but it will accept them in preference to nothing at all and can quickly become almost as attached to them as it was to the original treasure.

For most infants, the cuddly is only used at bedtime, or when conditions are unusually stressful. It can be an enormous comfort, for example, when infants have to go into hospital, giving them something intensely familiar in an intensely unfamiliar environment. If, at some stage, infants or toddlers start using their cuddlies more than usual and demanding them during the daytime, this can act as a valuable stress-barometer for the parents, telling them that their offspring is under undue pressure, for a reason that is perhaps hidden from them in other respects. A very few infants reach the point where they insist on cuddlies being in permanent contact with them, and in those cases it is necessary to ask serious questions about their emotional state. Their need for security has clearly become excessive.

How Do Babies Play?

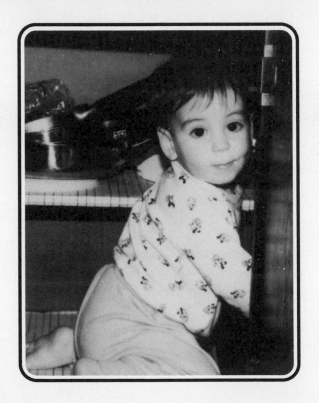

Many a newborn baby returns home to a nursery brimming with expensive toys. As a display of parental love, these are impressive but as far as the baby is concerned they are ahead of their time. They must await the toddler stage in the second year of life, after babyhood proper has ended, before they will have much significance. During the first year the baby's playful needs are much better fulfilled by gentle parental games than by the ingenious contents of modern toy shops.

During the first few weeks of life play is not important. The baby is still adjusting to its new existence outside the womb. Then, in the second month, it discovers the fun of watching exciting shapes moving about above its cot. Although it is stretching the definition a little, it could be said that *mobile-watching* is the first game that babies play. Parents who hang something that moves about in a slightly irregular, unexpected way, above the cot, will find that even at this tender age babies are fascinated by the changing positions of the shapes and will follow them closely with their eyes. Any objects that float through the air, as with a classic mobile, or which jiggle or flap when the baby shifts its body, will prove to be a source of intense interest. If the movement of the shapes repeats itself too often without variation, the interest will wane, however, demonstrating one of the basic laws of human play, namely that novelty is a key to playfulness.

At three months, *rattle-shaking* offers a new excitement. Anything that makes an unusual noise if it is accidentally hit or touched is appealing. If it can be held in the hand and waved about to create a strange sound, this is even more rewarding. Objects are investigated for their texture, shape, and color as well as the noise they produce, as the baby begins to explore the new world of "things."

It is playful interaction with the parent that gives the baby its greatest pleasures, and there are several characteristic games that develop at a very early age, all over the world. They include such delights as *funny face, peekaboo, gentle tickle,* and *vertigo*. The most important element in the baby's visual environment is the parental face, close up. Once it has learned to recognize the face of its own parents, somewhere between the ages of four and six months, it is ready for face games. It knows the face is friendly and so it can enjoy strange variations in that face. Parents find that making funny faces, or hiding their faces and then making them suddenly appear again, pleases the baby. It is enjoying the discovery that familiar things are flexible and can undergo change. This means that they can have familiarity and novelty at the same time, which is another of the basic qualities of playful elements.

More physical experiences, such as being gently tickled or nuzzled, or the frighteningly enjoyable sensation of vertigo as parents lift babies up in the air or swing them from side to side, all provide the baby with the exploratory excitements of learning about their sensations, their balance and the force of gravity. Little by little, through play of this kind, the baby starts to paint a mental picture of itself in its new—and still mysterious—environment. Some parents play too little with their babies, others too strongly. There is little risk in overdoing it, because if the physical play becomes too intense or prolonged, the baby's expressions and sounds quickly signal the shift from pleasure to panic, and the parents can stop instantly. Playing too little is more of a problem because the baby is limited in the extent to which it can ask for more play. There used to be a strict regime for babies in which they were expected to lie in their cots or carriages for long periods of time on their own with little parental interaction, and supposedly to benefit from the rest and solitude. But today it is recognized that gentle, playful interaction with parents is of great importance to the mental development of babies, and it is difficult for them to get too much of this. Even at a very early age, they enjoy hearing rhythmic sounds such as lullabies and nursery rhymes. They may not understand a word but they are fascinated by the rhythm and the tones, and especially by the association of the sounds with the now familiar faces.

When they are left on their own, babies are not idle. They spend much time examining their own hands and as soon as they are capable of putting things in their mouths they employ their sensitive lips and gums as another way of investigating the feel of objects. In addition to this *hand-play* and *mouth-play,* one of their favorite early games is *bang-bang.* They make the wonderful discovery that if something is hit it may make a loud noise. In the water at bathtime, *splash-splash* is a happy variant of this. Inherent in actions of this kind is the baby's determination to discover just how strong it is and how much impact it can make on its environment. All through childhood it will find power plays of this kind absorbingly exciting. The play principle involved here is that of *magnified reward*. This principle states that the greater the response the infant gets in relation to the effort expended, the more pleasure it gains. To give a simple example—a gentle hit on a balloon produces a huge amount of movement in relation to the strength of the blow. This makes balloons more exciting to infants than, say, heavy balls which barely move at all if hit in the same way. Similarly, a small object that makes a big noise, out of all proportion to its appearance, is exciting. The reason is obvious enough: the object that provides a magnified reward makes the infant feel bigger and stronger than it really is.

This pleasure in power is a sobering aspect of infantile play. They love anything that makes a startling impact. *Knock-down* is a favorite early game. This consists of watching studiously while the fond parent carefully builds a tower of blocks or discs, and then striking it forcefully enough to topple it over. The joy of destruction precedes the joy of construction by several months. (Which perhaps justifies the thought that the joy of soldiers is more infantile than the joy of architects.)

At around six to seven months new play patterns become important. Babies enjoy encountering other babies at this age for the first time. They explore one another's bodies and take a close interest in one another's actions. They are fascinated by seeing themselves in mirrors at this age, although they cannot yet quite work out how the mirror functions. *Hide-and-seek* also becomes popular, starting out with the "half-hidden" toy, and then progressing to full hiding.

Gymnastics become increasingly exciting and can be greatly aided by such devices as the *baby-bouncer*, a suspended sling-chair which enables the infant to kick down with its legs and feel itself bumping up into the air.

As babyhood comes to an end, games such as *pick-it-up*, another power play, arrive on the scene. In this, perspiring parents are repeatedly persuaded to replace thrown toys and any other small objects that happen to be within grabbing distance. Games of this type have a double power reward: not only is the object itself sent flying, but the parent is also sent bending. A more cooperative version is *give-and-take* in which objects are handed to parents and must then be handed back. This exchange ritual develops into more complicated games such as *post-box,* where small objects have to be inserted into large ones, until they have all gone, or *dismantling,* where complex objects are taken to pieces bit by bit.

As a prelude to the great day when babyhood ends, and the infant starts to walk unaided, there are several kinds of pre-walking games, such as playful locomotion with *pushalong toys.* The pushalongs are designed so that they cannot topple over on to the infant if it falls.

In all these games and with all these toys, the presence of the parent increases the value of the play immeasurably, not only as a participant, but also as a watcher. The watcher is more than a guardian and protector; he or she is also a witness to be impressed, an audience to applaud, and a companion with whom the baby can enjoy sharing the supreme pleasures of infantile play.

How Soon Can Babies Crawl?

S ome young animals can run about freely on the day they are
born, but the human baby must be patient. Locomotion takes
about six months to achieve. Body movements develop gradually in
a more or less predictable sequence. The first really efficient mode
of progression, that of crawling on the hands and knees, comes at
the end of a long series of lesser movements.

At the beginning, babies are incapable of moving themselves
from A to B. Their earliest actions are gentle hand movements,
usually investigating and fondling the mother's breast. Out of these
clumsy movements grow grasping, squeezing, and rubbing motions,
as the infant begins to discover the differences between things that
are rough or smooth, warm or cold, hard or soft.

Whole body movements during these earliest weeks are limited
largely to squirming or wriggling actions when the baby is disturbed
or upset. Eventually it does manage to shift the body a little way by
digging in the heels and then kicking out. This shoots it forward
and, although quite unorganized, is the first body movement that is
observed.

By the age of one month, babies can lift their chins off the ground if they are placed on their fronts. The action seems to represent an objection to being put in this position and is the best they can do to try and avoid it. Proper head control does not arrive until about three months of age. Shortly after this, the hands become more active, capable of reaching out for and grasping small objects. Before long these objects are carried by the hand to the mouth, which is used to investigate the feel of anything portable. The next step is to extend this object-to-mouth routine to include foot-to-mouth, the baby grabbing one of its feet and pressing its toes between its lips.

Then at the age of about four months comes the first real sign of pre-crawling. The baby starts to push upward with its arms, as if attempting infantile push-ups. By five months, it is capable of sustaining both this chest-up posture and also a bottom-up posture, but not at the same time. It is as if the infant has managed to perform the two halves of crawling but without being able to combine them into a true, progressive crawl. At about the same time it discovers how to roll over and may even use this as a crude form of limited progression.

At six months the baby can perform an "airplane" position, raising both its arms and legs off the ground together as it lies on its tummy. The body may even be rocked back and forth in this posture. At about the same time it may demonstrate "slithering"— dragging itself along on its tummy, using both arms and legs, but without much forward pace.

At seven months the baby's body becomes stronger in the middle and, at last, it is capable of sitting up unaided, in a well-controlled way. Finally, at about eight months of age, the infant performs its first crawl, with both chest and tummy up off the ground and its progression achieved by alternating movements of the arms and legs. The legs are bent and the main work is done, not by the hands and feet, but by the hands and knees. The first attempts are not always particularly impressive, especially as babies find it easier to crawl backward rather than forward. This is very frustrating when the toy they seek is in front of them, and they have to go through some careful trial-and-error movements until the desired forward progression is achieved.

Once proper crawling has arrived it develops fast during the ninth to twelfth months. Mobility is a great joy to the baby. It has an overpowering urge to explore and soon becomes amazingly adept at rapid disappearing acts in search of some exciting new stimulus. In fact, crawling is so rewarding that it tends to hold back the next momentous development—that of walking. But not for long. In a few months crawling will suddenly become an almost forgotten favorite, an old pattern of behavior that resurfaces only under special circumstances. And then, as the bravely bipedal child strides out into the world, it is gone forever.

How Soon Can Babies Walk?

B y my definition, when a baby can walk it is no longer a baby. The unaided act of walking marks the end of babyhood and it usually comes at the end of the first year of life. The exact time varies from child to child and the range of ages for first solo walking is generally put at between ten months and sixteen months. If an infant is not walking alone by the time it is eighteen months old, then it is necessary to check for possible hidden defects.

Walking does not appear suddenly, of course. It arrives in gradual stages. Stage one is extremely odd. This occurs when the newborn is only a few days old. If the tiny baby is supported vertically by the parental hands so that its feet are just in contact with a hard surface, the little legs press down strongly and start kicking out as if the infant is trying to stride boldly forward. These are reflex actions. They are automatic and cannot be modified or controlled in any way. Why they occur is a mystery, but they clearly herald the locomotory future of the tiny human and boldly state that "I am programmed as a walker."

At this stage the newborn is weak-of-limb and very top-heavy, with its comparatively huge head on its puny body. No matter how much exercise or training it gets, there is no hope of achieving a proper, independent walking action for many months. In fact, in stage two, the early reflex leg actions have vanished. They disappear after about fourteen days. If a one-month-old baby is held in the vertical position with its feet just touching the hard surface, instead of trying to stride out and kick its legs, it simply sags at the knees. The old, instinctive response has faded; the new, advanced response has yet to appear.

Stage three arrives at about three months of age (but sometimes as late as six months). Now, when supported on a hard surface, the baby's knees no longer sag and bend. The stubby legs are more determined. They stiffen and straighten trying to take the weight of the body. As the weeks pass, they become better and better at this, until the supported figure can stand erect and survey its new domain.

Between six and nine months of age, stage four arrives. This is the furniture epoch, when the baby uses any large object available to pull itself up into a vertical position. It usually has a favorite spot for doing this and stands there, rather proudly, clinging on to the furniture and looking around. It now discovers a basic truth about climbing, namely that it is often easier to get up than it is to get down. Like many a stranded kitten in an apple tree, it cannot solve the problem of returning to the safety of the ground. Inevitably these first, brave, independent hoistings into the upright position end with a bump. The infant collapses downward suddenly and thumps on to the ground. Despite this momentary setback, it is soon clambering up again, and again, until its legs have become used to the strange sensation of supporting all its body weight.

Stage five now develops. Between the ages of nine and twelve months, real forward walking arrives on the scene, but as yet it is always with adult aid. The hand is held tightly by the parent as the first faltering forward steps are taken. This generates great excitement and some frustration. Tottering forward and then losing balance is a common event. With each attempt the tottering becomes more controlled, more disciplined, and then finally, the great moment has arrived: stage six, the solo walk, usually with a proud parent crouching on the far side of the room with arms outstretched. The joy of achieving this stage is obvious, as if some deep-seated human destiny has been fulfilled. And so it has, for our prolonged bipedal walking gait is unique among mammals. Of all the 4,237 mammalian species alive today, human beings are the only true walkers. Kangaroos are bipedal, but they hop; bears and some apes can rear up and stagger a few paces, but they cannot walk for any distance. Walking is the most truly human of all our biological features.

Interestingly, the ability to walk survives even the most restrictive of childhood regimes. In some cultures babies have been restrained in an extreme way for generations. Certain tribes and societies have employed hard boards, to which infants are strapped for long periods of time. Attached to these carrying boards for purposes of easy transportation, these unfortunate babies were only released for bathing and other vital actions. The result, needless to say, was that they did not develop normal muscular movements. They were unable even to crawl, leave alone walk, at the age of one year. But as soon as they were released from this infant bondage, they rapidly caught up with other children. Although temporarily retarded in their muscular abilities, they soon made up for lost time. This demonstrates that, within each baby there is an unfolding, maturing process taking place and that hardly anything can stop it.

How Well Can Babies Swim?

For many years it was believed that babies could not swim and that they were always at risk near water. There were too many perfectly genuine and tragic examples of infants drowning in shallow garden ponds for anyone to doubt it. Even careful tests with babies gently lowered into warm, welcoming water resulted in wild thrashing about, spluttering, coughing, grabbing arms, and panic. It seemed clear that babies and water did not mix, but in the 1930s some more thoughtful research was carried out, with startling results. There was no doubt about it—handled correctly, newborn babies could swim.

The key discovery was that everything depended on the way the baby was placed in the water. In the earlier tests the infant had always been lowered in as though it were going to be given a bath. In other words it was lowered into the water in the faceup position. When all its body except for its face was submerged, it began to show signs of distress and to fling its arms and feet about as if trying to cling on to something to save itself. If its face was lowered right under the water, complete panic followed and it had to be removed quickly. The new tests tried a different method. In these the babies were placed in the water facedown and gradually submerged. This worked like magic. Instead of struggling violently they simply lay calmly in the water. They remained in their prone position and, without coughing or spluttering, they held their breath. They went on holding their breath and, with their eyes fully open below the surface, started to make reflex swimming movements. If allowed, with great care, to move independently of adult hands, their little swimming actions propelled them through the water. Even at only a few weeks of age, babies showed well integrated forward swimming of this type, revealing for the first time that, at this very tender age, the human baby is a natural swimmer. Clearly, it needs very close human supervision, very warm water, and the absence of harsh chemicals such as chlorine that could hurt the wide open eyes. But given the right conditions, newborn babies seem to be much better organized at aquatic locomotion than terrestrial. If they are held up in the air in the prone position, they will also make the alternating swimming movements, but they are then far less rhythmic and well-organized. The moment the babies go beneath the surface the movements flow more smoothly and become more synchronized. It looks very much as though humans can swim before they are able to walk or even to crawl.

Unfortunately there is a catch. The newborn swimming ability does not last. It vanishes in just a few months. If babies who are four months old are placed in water and tested in exactly the same way as the newborns, they panic no matter which position is used. If they are placed in the water facedown, they are calm for a moment but then start to rotate until they are in a faceup position. At this point they begin to struggle and panic sets in. They try to clutch hold of the nearby adult, they wipe their faces as if trying to remove the water from them, they sink deeper and they swallow water. All this happens very quickly and they have to be rescued almost immediately. And these are the same babies who, some weeks earlier, were propelling themselves cheerfully around the pool!

If infants are tested again when they are a few years old, instead of only a few months, the situation changes once more. Now, if they are placed carefully in the water in a prone position, they start trying to swim in a new way. Instead of the automatic, reflex swimming, they now attempt to *learn* swimming. Their actions are deliberate and voluntary. They are also less rhythmic and organized. From this point onward, with the help of inflatable floats, they can gradually accustom themselves to the water and by the time they are about four years old—if they have had daily access to water—will be able to swim unaided for short distances.

To sum up, there are three distinct phases of swimming for the young human: "early natural," "transitional panic," and "learned skill." The first, which operates from birth to the age of three or four months, is the automatic, instinctive phase. It is as though the baby is operating with the lower centers of its brain and propelling itself through the water like most other young mammals would do. When they are newly born, most other mammals react to water with precisely the same movements and the same inhibition of breathing while submerged, even if they are not aquatic species.

The obvious conclusion is that they are enjoying a brief "return to the womb," but it is not quite this simple. They do not have to actively suppress breathing when they are in the amniotic fluid because they have not yet started to breathe with their lungs. So the suppression of breathing while submerged is something new and rather special. Also, although the liquid medium may have an attractively familiar feel to it and may, as a result, produce a feeling of calm, the swimming actions performed cannot be explained as "fetus-like." The baby in the womb does not have room to swim about.

Although the liquid, womb-like quality of the water may explain the calm that enables swimming to take place, it cannot explain the controlled breathing or the synchronized movements of the limbs. These are something new and suggest that what we are seeing here is a glimpse of an earlier condition of the human being, at some primeval stage of our evolution. It has been claimed that we were once much more aquatic than we are today. Perhaps these newborn swimming actions hark back to those days and show how we once were—completely at home in the water.

What happens in the second half of babyhood is that this earlier "primitive" reaction vanishes as the higher centers of the thinking brain begin to become better developed and more dominant. Now the baby starts thinking and is quickly in trouble. The inborn trust of the water dwindles and disappears and it takes several years for the "thinking infant" and the toddler to regain that trust, not through instinct but through acquired skill. The changeover from the ancient to the more advanced behavior system can be a dangerous time, with instincts fading and skills as yet unlearned. It is during this phase—the second half of babyhood—that parental care is so essential and when, if infants are unobserved, there can be tragedies.

One intriguing side issue connected with the "water baby" phenomenon is the recent vogue for delivering babies under water. Water births in special birthing tanks have been carried out successfully in Russia, Germany, France, Britain, and the United States. The oddity of the procedure and the fears of newborns drowning have prevented this type of delivery from becoming widespread, but the adventurous parents who have tried it—under expert supervision—have reported that the birth is much more comfortable for the mother and far less stressful for the baby. The latest designs of birth pool enable the mother to adopt a more vertical posture, giving her the extra advantage of the force of gravity working for her. The delivery is far less painful and the mother much more relaxed. The newborn emerges into very warm water, an environment that is much closer to that in the womb. This enables it to take on its new challenges one at a time instead of explosively, all at once. After it has recovered from the shock of being squeezed through the birth canal, it can be gently brought up to the breast, where it can find the nipple. Moved gradually up out of the water, it can then, in the secure embrace of its mother, start to tackle the question of air-breathing. Its umbilical cord will go on beating for several minutes after birth, so there is no need to rush this phase. The newborn's natural inhibition about breathing under water stops it from trying for its first breath until it is clear of the surface. Those who have experienced this type of labor say that it seems to remove all urgency from the act of delivery. The mother's body "opens like a flower" and the buoyancy of the water gives her far more energy and more mobility as the baby is born. Despite its advantages to both mother and baby, many doctors dislike this type of labor because it is more difficult for them to take charge of the events that occur inside the pool. If the birth is a normal, healthy one, their objections are groundless, but if complications are likely, that is another matter. With modern technology, however, it should not be too difficult to predict what kind of delivery to expect and to act accordingly.

What Is a
Spoiled Baby?

A spoiled baby is one who has been disciplined, not one who
has been pampered. This is the precise opposite of the usual
definition and requires some explanation.

It has often been said that when a baby cries it is "trying to get
the better of you" or "trying to rule your life," as though it were
some tiny scheming creature out to trick you. In earlier days it was
commonplace to ignore the screams of a miserable infant and to
wait for the sobbing to die down. Crying was often described as the
baby "exercising its lungs." It was thought of as some kind of natural
and inevitable breathing routine or vocal development. If mothers
felt tempted, by their natural instincts, to go to their babies, they
were sternly told to resist this temptation and leave the crying
infant strictly alone. It was pointed out that if a baby crying in the
night was left to itself it would cry slightly less on each subsequent
night and, in this way, the parents could train it to leave them in
peace when they wanted to sleep.

The appeal of this argument led to many parents following the
recommended routine, even though they might find the screaming
heartrending at first and have to cover their ears. And it worked.

The crying did become reduced. But this was like breaking a horse. The baby's natural call for help was being destroyed by repeated lack of reward. Deep down in its mind it concluded that its parents were not, after all, the great protectors and defenders that its instincts had led it to believe. Its trust in them was eroded. In the true sense it was being spoiled.

Babies are so physically helpless and vulnerable that what they need during the first year of life is total and complete caring and comforting. They are too young to benefit from strict routines and firm discipline. Of course, at a much later stage, when the young child starts to explore its world, often injudiciously, it needs and does indeed benefit from some degree of discipline. The toddler that runs out into the middle of a busy road will soon die without such discipline. But babies are different.

The baby that is cossetted and cuddled, cooed over and comforted, is the one that will be most likely to grow into a tough adult. The sternly disciplined baby may well end up as the shy and insecure individual in later life. This is because the protected baby learns, right from the start, that it is worthy of attention. It senses that it is loved and therefore that it must be lovable. With this inner strength it sets forth to investigate the world and explore its ever-expanding horizons. It grows up to become an outward-going child because it has behind it the secure sensation of having been totally loved.

For the overdisciplined baby the future is more threatening. It has learned that life can be cruel, that it can experience complete helplessness without finding a protective hand to support it, or an arm to embrace it. For the loved baby, the motto of childhood becomes "nothing ventured, nothing gained"; for the disciplined baby the motto becomes "nothing ventured, nothing lost."

To sum up, a spoiled schoolchild may well be one who has been disciplined too little, but a spoiled baby is one who has been disciplined too much.

Are Babies Intelligent?

S trictly speaking, no, they are not. The correct definition of intelligence is that it is the ability to combine past experiences to solve new problems. Babies simply do not have enough experiences to be able to recombine them into new solutions. And most of their problems are solved for them by their parents. Even if some problems are not dealt with by their protectors, there is little that babies can do about them because their bodies are too clumsy to implement the solutions.

It is important not to confuse intelligence with other mental qualities. Babies may not be intelligent, but if they are healthy and well cared for they are extremely alert and highly sensitive to the minute-by-minute stimulation that bombards their waking hours from the moment of delivery to the moment they leave babyhood behind and become walking, talking toddlers. They are like sponges—soaking up their new world and learning its basic properties and natural laws.

Throughout the first year of life, babies are busy laying the foundations for what will one day make them adult members of the most intelligent of all the 1,124,000 species of animals alive on the planet today. They arrive well equipped with sensory powers and a set of crucial inborn responses. These enable the newborn babies to enlist the loving care of their adult protectors. They do not need "cunning" to do this, as has been claimed in the past. The suggestion of cunning implies that they are lying in their cots scheming and plotting the best way to dominate their parents. Such views, popular in earlier decades, were used as the excuse for attempting to introduce disciplinary regimes for babies as a means of controlling and defeating their "fiendish attempts" to exploit adults. This led to endless mistreatment of babies and a gross misunderstanding of what it means to have a baby's mind.

The instinctive reactions of human babies—such responses as sucking at the breast, crying when in distress, smiling and laughing as a way of prolonging intimacy with parents—are enough to keep them safe in any typical family context (providing, of course, that the adults involved have not been brainwashed into resisting their *own* inborn reactions to their babies). One particularly important quality of the human baby is its ability to learn. Endowed with its good range of sensory capacities—hearing, vision, taste, touch, smell, balance, and temperature detection—the baby can start to monitor the outside world and learn how it is organized. At first, the utilization of its memory is extremely poor and does not show any marked improvement until after the baby phase is almost over. This might appear to make learning impossible. How can one learn something if one cannot remember it? The answer seems to be that the learning process in the alert, playful baby is more a matter of collecting impressions than acting on them. To give an analogy, if a shopper goes to the supermarket and buys large stores of foods, takes them home and puts them in the freezer, that freezer is well stocked, even if the shopper cannot remember what was bought. The brain of the alert baby becomes well stocked with impressions, even though it may not be able to recall them precisely.

Whether the brain of a baby will be able to develop normally if it is starved of input is a hotly debated point. Some authorities believe that the growth of brain power will continue with its own momentum, regardless of the degree of external stimulation, while others insist that an exciting environment with a great deal of social, mental, and physical stimulation is essential to produce a brilliant adult. The truth is difficult to obtain but probably lies between these two extremes. Babies are remarkably resilient. The unstimulated baby will be able to make up for lost time as it grows up. No matter what happens to it, if it survives it will have the potential to become a viable adult. But will it suffer from adult neuroses and perhaps some inadequacies? It might turn out to be a successful adult, but could it have developed into a happier, more balanced one if its babyhood had been more loving and stimulating? This remains one of the great mysteries of the growth of human personality.

Whatever the precise truth about the development of individual intelligence, it does seem like simple common sense to suggest that, if an infant enjoys a playful, active babyhood, it will have the best chance of becoming an adventurous adult. We may not be able to prove that a boring babyhood creates a less intelligent adult, but why take the risk?

Are Babies Left-handed or Right-handed?

I n any group of human adults the majority are always right-handed. The figures vary slightly, but approximately only one person in every ten is left-handed. This applies to all races and cultures everywhere in the world and at all times in history, as far as we can tell. Judging by the tools he left behind, even Stone Age man was already favoring his right hand. But what about babies? How soon does the right-handed bias start to show itself?

According to a recent statement published by the British Health Education Authority: "Most children use both their right and left hands, without preference, until about three years old." Casual observation seems to support this view. One day, the baby reaches out with its left hand to grasp an offered toy; some weeks later the right hand is used. The obvious conclusion is that the baby has not yet "settled down" to its adult preference and is essentially ambidextrous. But this is only a half-truth. The whole truth is more complicated and much more interesting.

A more detailed study has revealed that the human infant goes through a whole series of shifts from left-bias to right-bias as it grows older. The sequence is as follows:

1. At twelve weeks of age, babies respond to an offered object by moving both their arms about. The movements usually alternate, first one hand becoming more active, then the other. There is little or no bias at this age and the arm movements do not yet lead to contact with the object. Controlled reaching out and grasping is yet to come.

2. At sixteen weeks of age, babies have started to make contact with offered objects, reaching out for them with one hand. At this stage, the majority prefer to use the *left* hand, regardless of whether they will, as adults, become left-handed or right-handed. Intriguingly, babies sometimes make a sudden switch from one hand to the other when they are halfway through a test session, and once they have done this, they then stay with their "second" hand choice. It is as if they are exploring both possibilities, checking to see which one is better.

3. At twenty weeks of age, babies cease to show these shifts during the test sessions. They are now strongly unilateral and their one-sidedness continues to show a *left* bias.

4. At twenty-four weeks of age, the strong bias is lost and there is typically a bilateral, two-handed approach to offered objects.

5. At twenty-eight weeks of age, babies are unilateral again and now the *right* hand is the most commonly used. But although this is usually the dominant hand, at this stage there is a great deal of variety in reaching actions. Sometimes there is again a shift halfway through an observational session, with the other hand being brought into play, or even some two-handed actions being performed. The baby is still exploring its options, but is nevertheless predominantly right-handed.

6. At thirty-two weeks of age, the bilateral, two-handed approach returns.

7. At thirty-six weeks the bilateral actions are less common and a bias reappears, this time toward the *left* hand once more. There is now far less chance of this bias changing during a test session.

8. At forty weeks of age, babies are now strongly unilateral and the *right* hand has become the dominant one in most cases. The same is true at forty-four weeks.

9. At forty-eight weeks there is a temporary switch back to the *left* hand in some babies, but the right hand continues to predominate.

10. At fifty-two weeks there is a clear dominance of the right hand in most babies.

Although this is the end of "babyhood," the growing infant has still more shifts to make. At eighty weeks there is confusion and a great deal of bilateral behavior again. At two years of age, the right hand dominates once more. But then, between two and a half and three and a half years of age, infants go through one last phase of bilateral actions before, at about four years, settling down to a characteristic dominant hand. This bias then becomes stronger and stronger until at roughly eight years of age the child has acquired what will become its lifelong adult form of handedness.

Once again, these detailed observations underline just how complex and fascinating the human baby is. Far from being "without preference," as the Health Education Authority would have us believe, handedness goes through what can best be described as a series of pendulum swings from left to right to left, as the infant passes through its first year of life. It is as if it is trying out first one hand and then the other one, to establish, over a period of months, which one makes it feel more comfortable when examining objects offered to it by an adult. But why is its first bias toward the left and its final choice more to the right? To understand this we must take a look at the way other primates behave.

Tests with monkeys and apes have proved that they show a slight but distinct bias toward the left, when using their hands. Observations of free-living Japanese macaque monkeys revealed that, of those showing a bias (and 40 percent did not), two out of every three were left-handed. So, when human babies, at sixteen weeks, start to show a left-handed bias, they are, perhaps, performing a primeval primate action. The human bias for the right then starts to take over and, by twenty-eight weeks has literally gained the upper hand. The battle between the ancient primate left and the modern human right then proceeds to tug the growing baby this way and that until, after some years, the child has settled down in the majority of cases to become right-handed.

Because, in evolutionary terms, this right-bias is a comparatively recent development it has yet to reach the 100 percent level that we may one day expect to see. We know from studies of Stone Age hand-axes, that the right bias for humans, although well established 200,000 years ago, was not as strong as it is today. Of axes that showed a bias, 65 percent appear to have been fashioned by right-handed individuals. The biggest study of handedness in modern times was carried out in the United States in 1953 when 12,159 army recruits were tested and 91.4 percent proved to be right-handed. So, since the Stone Age it would seem that the swing to the right has become stronger and stronger and there is no reason to suppose that the trend has finished. What our babies reflect with their pendulum swings from left to right is the struggle that has gone on in the past to convert the ancient monkey bias to the new and opposite human preference. We see in their gradual progression the triumph of the new hand-dominance over the old one.

This may describe what has happened, but it does not tell us why it has happened. Most authorities sidestep this question without even attempting an answer. Long ago, Thomas Carlyle dismissed the query as to why the right hand was chosen as "not worth asking except as a kind of riddle." But it *is* worth asking because the bias is so strange. Why are we not 50/50 left and right? Obviously, with our evolution as tool-makers and implement-users we had to specialize and let one hand become dominant in each individual, but why do nine out of ten people choose the same, right hand? And if so many of them do this, then why not all of them?

The anatomy of the baby gives us a few clues. Even before birth, the right side of the body is slightly favored by the human nervous system. There are more nerves leading from the brain to the right side of the body than to the left. Also, within a few hours of birth, human babies show stronger electrical activity in the side of the brain that controls the right side of the body. In addition, it has been discovered that 60 percent of babies lie in the womb with their right sides closer to their mother's body surface. This could mean that the right sides of these babies receive more stimulation during pregnancy, and in this way become slightly more "advanced." It is also claimed that as early as the twenty-ninth week of gestation the two halves of the brain have already developed a degree of asymmetry favoring the left hemisphere—the hemisphere that controls the right side of the body. This half of the brain is said to exhibit a stronger development in one portion of the left temporal lobe and this again may favor the right hand later in life.

These are all indications that the right side will have slightly stronger chances of becoming dominant, but it still begs the question as to why *right* and not *left*. A left-handed spear-thrower can aim just as accurately and propel his weapon just as powerfully as a right-handed warrior, so why are there nine right-handed spear-throwers out of every ten men?

To answer this we must look for some other kind of asymmetry in human behavior that might influence the right bias. As mentioned later, the majority of women cradle their babies in their left arms, unconsciously bringing the young one's ear close to their beating heart and the sound that soothes and calms all babies. This is done by most mothers, regardless of whether they are themselves left- or right-handed. Therefore most babies will, by turning their heads to the right, gain maternal rewards—milk, warmth, comforting, contact, and protection. So the right swing of the head is, for most babies, a more attractive action than a left swing. This seems to have exerted a strong influence on a neck habit called the "tonic neck reflex." The reflex is seen whenever a baby is lying on its front. In this prone position, the one head posture that the baby cannot adopt—without suffocating—is the symmetrical face-down position. It *must* rotate its head to one side or the other. And its preference for a right turn of the head, already established at birth means that it is more likely to perform a right neck-twist than a left one. The right neck-twist is always accompanied by an asymmetry of the limbs as the baby lies on its front. This asymmetry may then contribute to the long-term preference for one hand becoming dominant. So it could well be this infantile neck-bias linked to the mother's cradling actions that lead ultimately to the right-handedness of humans.

Why then are there still so many left-handers remaining today? The answer seems to be that left-handers are reverting to the more primitive primate condition and are not, for some reason, getting the "new" human influences in their early development. In other words they are not, perhaps, enjoying the cradling bias to the same extent. Circumstances that could influence this might be: difficult births that affect the mother's health; periods of social stress, such as wartime, depression, or revolt, where the maternal peace and calm is repeatedly put under severe stress; or the presence of twins that makes it difficult or impossible to offer left-sided cradling of the usual kind. If the incidence of left-handers increases in these cases, then it would seem that the left-cradling explanation is valid. And that is precisely what has been found. Left-handed individuals do show a marked increase where there have been difficult births, stressful social conditions, or the presence of twins.

This explanation seems to make much more sense than the more usual one which describes the "lefties" as social rebels—individuals who refuse to follow the herd and insist on being different. That argument is repeatedly put forward, but careful observations of babies soon make it clear that handedness is something that precedes all forms of "social rebellion" and is a pattern of behavior that is established long before we are aware of it. True, in authoritarian cultures, where for some religious or superstitious reason, left-handedness is rigorously suppressed in schools, only the out-and-out rebels will be prepared to fight against the tyranny of the right-handers. But in many other cultures where there is no such pressure and children are allowed to follow whichever hand-bias they prefer, the left-handers exist as a clearly nonrebellious minority group, usually rather puzzled at the way their bodies demand a left-sided preference. There, the rebel explanation is inadequate.

How Important Is the Mother to Her Baby?

© 1991 by Whitney Lane

This may sound like a ridiculous question, but in recent years there have been a number of voices raised in opposition to the idea of natural motherhood. Certain feminists, who protect their ideals by stubbornly ignoring the anthropological evidence, have suggested that the human "family unit" is a cunning trick played by men on unsuspecting women. They believe that it is a very recent invention, no more than 10,000 years old, and that it emerged out of the agricultural revolution, a revolution that saw male farmers looking upon all adult females, whether human or otherwise, as useful breeding machines.

According to this theory of non-motherhood, women are not naturally child-loving and instinctively maternal. They are conditioned to this idea by social pressures put upon them by the dominant males of society. The theory fosters the notion that shared parental duties, with whole groups of individuals looking after babies, are more natural for our species. Babies can be brought up communally by specialists, leaving the mothers free to wander the corridors of power.

For some women this doctrine has obvious appeal, but is it well based in biological fact? Do mothers matter to their babies, as so many traditionalists believe, or will any caring adults do just as well? There are only two ways to find out. One is to make direct observation of mothers with their babies and the other is to run a check on the ultimate fate of babies that have been brought up on the communal, non-family system.

Direct observations reveal that, in truth, both mother and baby work hard to strengthen the bond that grows naturally between them. For the first three months, on average, babies do not mind particularly who looks after them, although they are already starting to differentiate the smell, look, and sound of their "special minder." By the time they have reached about four months they are suddenly very choosy, screaming at strangers and seeking the company only of their mothers (or whichever individual has accepted the primary responsibility for rearing them). Similarly, mothers respond more and more strongly to their own babies, as distinct from other infants. The bond tightens until extreme distress is felt by either party if forced separation occurs. The strong feelings involved in this bonding process are often irrational in their intensity and, to a biologist, look exactly like those observed in other "family-unit" species. The suggestion that the baby is pushed into wanting one maternal figure, or that the mother is driven to care for her child by a sense of guilt and social responsibility is ludicrous to anyone who has witnessed or felt the depth of the emotions involved.

The opponents of this view immediately point out the high incidence of battered babies, abandoned infants, and other evidence of non-maternal mothers. Divorce and infidelity are brought in to the argument and it is insisted that the family unit is held together, rather weakly, from the *outside* and not from any powerful internal bonds of attraction that might be laid down in our ancient genetic programming. In making such criticisms an obvious fact is overlooked, namely that our human populations today are wildly overcrowded and that when other species are subjected to similar overpopulation they too exhibit a collapse in the family-unit breeding system. Overcrowd even the most devoted species sufficiently and you will see a growing maelstrom of family chaos. Babies are killed, eaten, raped, abandoned, and starved, where once they were fed, cleaned, warmed, and protected. Pair-bonds fragment where once they were faithful and caring. So we must not expect miracles from the human family unit, just because it is a biologically programmed aspect of our behavior.

Ultimately, of course, the proof of the rival theories lies in the behavior of the babies when they become adults. Are the family-raised babies more successful as adults than the group-raised ones? If a baby has a mother-figure (technically referred to as a "reference person") dominating its infancy, does such a baby live a fulfilled social life as an adult, or does it become one of the antisocial minority? One place to test this is in our modern prisons. There, undeniably, we have a human sample with a strong bias toward the antisocial and the unsuccessful. What does a survey of prison inmates tell us about child rearing?

A study has recently been carried out in certain European prisons and there it was discovered that a much higher proportion than usual of the population had experienced a deprived or abused childhood. In 1977, for example, the figure was as high as 34 percent in one prison. When the prisoners were investigated for "reference persons," it was discovered that 95 percent of them had *not* enjoyed the love of a central mother-figure during their babyhood. As infants they had, for one reason or another, been looked after by a confusing series of adult minders. Before their childhood was over, 50 percent of them had been subjected to more than five changes in "mother-figure."

These findings are a powerful condemnation of modern theories that see motherhood as a culturally invented trap. Clearly, motherhood is of fundamental importance to the developing baby. The infant, as it starts to identify individuals *as* individuals, desperately needs to focus its dependency on one dominant figure to which it will always turn for care and protection, whenever it feels insecure or unsure of the strangely changing world it encounters. The human baby comes into the world pre-programmed for this focusing and without it the delicate balance of the growing mind of the child becomes all too easily disturbed. Infants forced by circumstances to survive without a specific mother-figure do not, of course, die. They struggle to adapt, but in so doing they accumulate problems for themselves in later days. They grow up physically strong but mentally bruised. They may find it difficult to make lasting attachments as adults. Their trust in loyalty may be blunted. They sometimes lack feelings of guilt and become crudely or even cruelly insensitive in their dealings with other adults. This does not happen in every case. Many individuals do manage to defeat the problem, but it will always be a greater struggle for them than for those babies who grew up in a typical family unit with all the gentle, close intimacies that that involves.

Why Are Babies Swaddled?

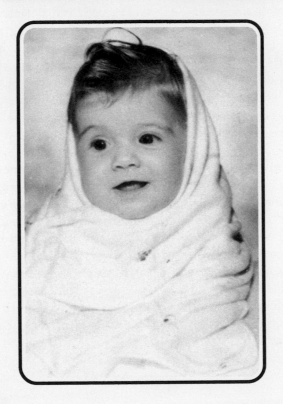

When the baby is inside the womb its body is permanently embraced by its mother's flesh. This enfoldment gives it protection and safety. When it is born it suddenly loses this condition and, as its skin feels the outside air, it senses the absence of security and it panics. Only if its mother embraces it with her arms and holds it to her warm, soft body, can it be calmed. But she cannot keep this up. If she were a monkey or an ape, it would be easy, because her newborn would be able to cling tightly to her coat of fur and remain attached for as long as necessary. The tight embrace would last and last, keeping the infant calm and relaxed, even in the strange new, outside world. But the human baby cannot cling in this way. Its arms and legs are not strong enough and, even if they were, there is no coat of fur on to which it could attach itself. Its mother's body is smooth and slippery and it can only enjoy the tight embrace if she herself does all the work of holding on. She can do this for a while, but then some new form of enfoldment is needed to comfort the baby. The answer is to encase it in a warm soft sheath of clothing. If this is wrapped firmly around its body, it will re-create the sensation of being embraced, and the baby will quiet down and rest.

This is why, for thousands of years, babies have been swaddled during their earliest days. Because there has been a great deal of opposition to swaddling in recent years, some tests were carried out to discover whether or not swaddling really does have any beneficial effects. Using modern technology, doctors found that when babies are snugly wrapped up in soft, warm blankets or shawls, they do indeed have a slower heartbeat and slower, more steady respiration. In addition, they are less fretful, cry less, and sleep more. Unwrapped babies thrash around in a lively way, but they also happen to be more tense, more stressed, and much more fretful. So why did swaddling go out of fashion? To understand this it is necessary to look back at its early history.

As far back as the Early Bronze Age, over four thousand years ago, there are depictions of tightly swaddled babies. Prehistoric figurines show mothers holding in their arms infants that are strapped down to flat back boards. These carrying boards were portable cradles that the women could take with them as they moved about. They were working mothers who could not leave their infants behind and needed some way of transporting them from place to place as they gathered food or carried out their other duties. By wrapping the babies up in thick clothing and strapping them to the boards, they were able to keep them warm, calm, and safe. The boards could be attached to the mothers' backs when they walked and could then be hooked on to trees out of doors, or on to walls or ceilings when back at the family dwelling. In this way they were protected from hazards at ground level. Because of the tight binding, the infants remained calm and slept a great deal, almost as if they felt they were back in the womb once more. It was an efficient form of child care, given the primitive circumstances.

This kind of tight swaddling was widespread in many cultures, and for many centuries. It was commonplace in the ancient world. All the early Greeks and Romans were swaddled, and most Europeans as well, right up to the eighteenth century. Then a rebellion against the practice began. It was felt to be artificial and unnatural and was abandoned in favor of the "freedom of movement" regime. The "return to nature" demanded the immediate removal of the tight swaddling clothes. There has been strong support for this view, right down to the present day, with the kicking and thrashing of unwrapped babies seen lovingly as exploratory self-expression and the vigorous strengthening of young limbs and bodies, rather than as signs of anxiety and distress.

The new freedom school was not entirely stupid. The old methods had gone too far. We know this because, in certain remote parts of Asia, Central America, Russia, Eastern Europe, and Scandinavia, the ancient style of rather brutal strapping-down of babies survived until recent times. In a few areas it still goes on today. Studies of tribal societies revealed that the swaddling was often *so* tight that it was doing physical damage to some of the babies. It had become a tribal belief that the newborn had to be completely flattened against the carrying board in order to "keep the back straight." It was also believed that if the infant could move its arms and legs about freely it would damage its supposedly soft and poorly formed bones. This degree of "protection" sometimes caused the very damage it was supposed to prevent. Some babies were so enthusiastically flattened that they suffered from dislocated hips. It is hardly surprising that the old tradition of tight swaddling came under fire.

Unfortunately, as so often happens, when the pendulum of custom swings away from an old practice it swings too far in the opposite direction. This was the case here, and the "freedom school" removed not only the harmful aspects of swaddling, but also its beneficial effects. What the baby needs is a compromise. By using snug but loose swaddling, instead of the very tight wrapping, the modern baby can be given the feeling of security, but without in any way being physically damaged. The blanket or shawl is simply wrapped around the baby's body and it is then placed on a soft bed. The hard carrying board is no longer in evidence. The wrappings are firm enough to make the baby sleepy and relaxed, but not so firm that they cannot be kicked loose if the infant awakens and feels in need of a little vigorous exercise.

If the freedom-of-movement school argues that even this degree of wrapping up is too inhibitory and cramps the baby's natural development, then they must provide evidence to support their view, and this they do not seem to be able to do. In fact, there is some striking evidence against them. Investigators visited two of the countries where tight swaddling is still common today—Russia and Iraq—and examined the babies that had been subjected to the old "carrying board" treatment. In the West, the modern semi-swaddled babies are usually only wrapped up during their first few weeks. After that they move on to ordinary baby clothing. Not so in Russia and Iraq. There, the infants are swaddled throughout the whole of their first year—virtually their entire babyhood. Observers watched to see what happened when these babies were released from their tight wrappings at the age of one year. To their surprise they found that, *in a matter of hours,* these supposedly retarded infants were able to catch up with the body skills of babies that had been free during their early months. What this means is that the human nervous system forges ahead with its development regardless of the physical restraints of the carrying board. Practice and exercise of the infantile limbs is less important than one might imagine. The baby is an amazingly efficiently pre-programmed growing machine and even prolonged immobility does not seem to be able to halt or hamper its progress. Bearing in mind the fact that individuals such as Alexander the Great, Julius Caesar, and Jesus

Christ must all have been tightly swaddled as babies, this is not so surprising.

Despite these findings, there is no advantage in returning to the earlier form of very tight swaddling. If done badly, it is clearly dangerous and can in a few cases lead to bone damage. There is no point in taking the risk. Circumstances no longer demand the transportability of an immobilized infant, and we now know that softer swaddling is just as calming as tight binding. The compromise works. It is magically soothing for the more tense babies, and yet it permits the more energetically active babies to kick themselves free whenever they feel like it.

Why Do Babies
Like Being Rocked?

Every mother knows that rocking movements sooth a baby. An agitated baby can be made calm by rocking and a calm one can be sent to sleep. The rhythmic movements seem to work because they re-create some of the conditions the baby experienced when it was lying snugly inside its mother's womb. It is usually stated that it is the walking movements of the mother that are being re-created but it is not quite that simple.

It is certainly true that the motion of the rocking action can be explained as a reminder of the mother's walking, but the ideal speed for rocking is not the same as that for normal walking. Careful observations have revealed that rocking has the best effect when it is between sixty and seventy moves per minute, with each move being no more than about three inches. Also, the movement of the baby's body should be forward and backward rather than side to side. The rocks should be gentle, repetitive, and rhythmic, with no breaks in tempo, if they are to have the maximum calming effect. Most of these qualities are clearly related to the kind of sensation the fetus would experience before birth, as its mother moves about, but the speed is too slow. The average walking speed exceeds 100 paces per minute and so, for this feature, it is necessary to look for some other influence. The obvious answer appears to be the beating of the human heart. This averages about seventy-two beats a minute and is therefore much closer to the rocking speed.

So it seems that the fetus feels the movements and hears the beating of the maternal heart and that a combination of these sensations, re-created by rocking, has the best calming effect. The reason for this double influence is probably connected with the fact that the mother's heart keeps on beating incessantly, whereas walking stops and starts and varies its speed when the mother runs or strolls. So heartbeat speed is more strongly imprinted on the baby's memory than walking speed. Significantly, mothers who pace up and down when rocking their babies to sleep, slow their walking pace considerably. They reduce it from the usual brisk 100 + paces per minute to something much closer to sixty to seventy paces. They are, of course, quite unaware why they are doing this, but it feels right.

A few babies, when they reach the age of about nine months, may start rocking themselves. They sit up and sway their bodies back and forth, back and forth, for long periods of time. This self-rocking indicates a need for comfort and shows that these particular babies are not getting sufficient comfort from their parents or protectors. Such babies clearly need a great deal more loving body contact than they are receiving and their self-rocking should be taken seriously as a sign that all is not well.

How Is a Baby Transported?

T he human baby presents a special problem when being moved from place to place. Even in modern times, with clothes covering the mother's body, the baby's limbs are not strong enough to enable it to cling to her when she is walking, running, or working. As a result, a whole variety of carrying devices have been employed over the centuries.

Over short distances the baby can be carried in the parent's arms, but this soon becomes uncomfortable and inactivates the parent's hands. An alternative is to carry the baby on the hip, which at least leaves one arm free for action, but for complete freedom of the parental arms some kind of sling is necessary.

The simplest sling sees the baby clamped to one maternal hip, with the cloth passing over the mother's opposite shoulder. Since the times of ancient Egypt there has also been a frontal sling, one that passes around the mother's neck and clamps the baby to the front of her body. Some tribal peoples use a wide belt that straps the baby to one flank, as the mother toils at food collecting or preparation. Still others strap the baby to the back, with a modified cloak or skirt holding it in place and tying around the front of the mother's body.

A more advanced technique employs a swaddling board to which the baby is firmly strapped. This board is then worn as a backpack, tied to the mother by straps around her waist and over her shoulders. In some cultures the strap securing the board passes not over the shoulders but over the top of the head, resting in a recess in the mother's hair or headgear. This particular solution gives the impression of being rather painful for the maternal neck muscles, but its popularity over thousands of years and in a variety of cultures suggests that, in reality, it is more comfortable than it looks.

All of these methods were eventually to be replaced by the invention of the baby carriage by a Mr. Charles Burton in New York in 1848. This wheeled baby vehicle was not, however, an immediate success. Pedestrians hurrying along busy city streets were not ready for its sudden appearance. Collisions were frequent and anger rose to oppose this new-fangled obstruction. Instead of giving up the struggle, Burton abandoned New York and moved to London. There his fortunes changed dramatically when Queen Victoria ordered one of his baby carriages and overnight endowed it with high social status. Now mothers flocked to buy them and Burton's factory was kept busy trying to meet the demand. The "perambulator" was here to stay. By 1865 magazines were making perambulator jokes and one journalist painted a word-picture of this impressive new form of baby transport: "The perambulator has given us children, looking on with their grave smooth faces at the business of life, as they lean back philosophically in their carriages."

The baby carriage became more and more streamlined and sophisticated as the decades passed until eventually it evolved into the modern baby buggy. This lighter, more portable vehicle, invented in 1965, was easier to handle because it was collapsible and could be stored or taken into shops, cars, or trains.

Even more recently, a modern version of the baby sling has been reintroduced, with infants strapped to either the chest or the back of the free-striding parent. For more athletic mothers and fathers this return to ancient styles of baby transport is even more adaptable and may herald a step back to one of the most primitive solutions to the problem of human family mobility.

How Soon Can Babies Be Toilet-trained?

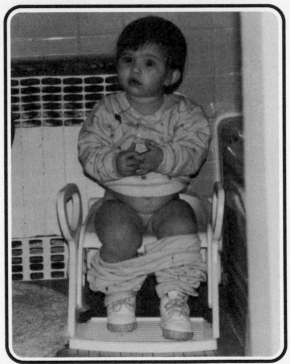

T he simple, unavoidable answer to this question is that babies cannot be toilet-trained. Remembering that I am defining a baby as a human infant during its first year of life, it is true to say that no baby is capable of voluntary control of either its urination or its defecation. During the first twelve months babies urinate and defecate automatically, as a reflex action, whenever their bladder or bowels sense a certain level of pressure. No matter how much the parents may try to organize and influence the timing of these actions, there is no hope of true control during the babyhood phase.

Despite this fact, many mothers try to impose some sort of discipline or conditioning on the toilet activities of their babies. Driven by the twentieth-century obsession with hygiene, they introduce various regimes prematurely. Amazingly, in one British study it was found that no fewer than 20 percent of mothers in one city attempted to toilet-train their babies from the first weeks of life. Over 80 percent had begun some sort of training before the babyhood phase was over. By contrast, in an American study, it was clear that hardly any mothers imposed training routines during the first year of life.

How do the babies fare in these premature routines? Some mothers claim a degree of success, but if babies are biologically incapable of controlling themselves, what exactly is taking place? The answer is what has been called "toilet timing." This gives the impression of being true training, but it is not. What happens is that babies are most likely to defecate and urinate after a meal. This is logical enough and so some mothers develop the habit of regularly placing their babies on pots immediately after feeding them. There is a strong chance that they will in this way catch the right moment and save themselves the trouble of a diaper change. But they are mistaken if they think the baby is cooperating with them in this endeavor. The baby is simply doing what it would do anyway, pot or no pot, and even if it senses that it is pleasing its mother it is incapable of fine-tuning its response or varying it in any way to suit her.

This timing process usually collapses toward the end of the baby period as the infant begins, at last, to control its functions. It now no longer reacts automatically after each meal and the mother becomes confused and worried. But what she is experiencing need not concern her. It is the start of true control. This phase is not usually completed successfully for some months. Voluntary sphincter control may be achieved as early as twelve to fifteen months, but eighteen months is more likely, and many children take much longer.

A detailed British study revealed that by the second year of life just over half (54 percent) of children were toilet-trained. By the third year of life the figure had risen to 93 percent. This applied to defecation. Urination control takes a little longer, and night urination control takes longer than day urination control.

These figures all relate to the period following babyhood, but one aspect is relevant here. The human baby matures at a more or less set rate. It is ready for new developments when *it* is ready and not before. No amount of parental anxiety or impatience will accelerate the process. Studies of children who have passed the baby phase and begun to control their toilet activities have been designed to see whether early, attempted toilet-training during babyhood has had any effect on later performance. The answer is that it does not seem to make the slightest difference. Efforts to impose early controls and disciplines on tiny babies neither hasten nor retard their later acquisition of toilet controls. Human development will take its own good time to deal with this important matter and there is nothing any eager parent can do about it.

If the early toilet-training becomes severe or frantic, it may, perhaps, lay down difficulties for later life, with deep-seated neuroses about defecation and urination lying dormant to resurface uncomfortably in older childhood or even in adult life. The best plan, in terms of human parental behavior, is to treat the whole business of toilet activities in a simple, down-to-earth manner. Speaking biologically it is perhaps not going too far to say "let the baby train itself." By about eighteen months of age the infant will start to *know* that it has soiled itself and will draw attention to this fact. It is then easy for the parent to help the toddler to solve its problem and the toddler will understand and cooperate. In other words, the parent does not try to lead the child but to follow it, in dealing with this issue. In this way the child will take the whole procedure as a simple matter of course, and not make a great drama out of it. Unfortunately many modern parents, especially city-dwellers (who lack the more casual approach to waste-matter typical of the countryman), cannot resist attempts to hurry their babies into a state of premature cleanliness.

The facts about waste products during the baby phase are as follows: The baby starts urinating even before it has left the mother's womb. The fetus does not, however, defecate in the womb. The first feces appear shortly after birth and are of a special kind, called meconium. This means literally "like opium-juice" and refers to their strange, dark, greenish-black color. After the newborn has become milkfed, its feces are a soft yellow color and appear between three and twelve times daily during the first weeks. At this stage the infant may urinate up to eighteen times a day. By the age of two to three months most babies will have reduced their defecations to two a day and by the end of babyhood, at the age of one year, they are nearly all down to the once a day level, even though they do not yet have voluntary control.

Anyone who has reared a small chimpanzee will know that its maturation process works in the same way. The difference is that the infant ape is nearly always clinging on to the body of the human foster-parent. When the ape is at its equivalent of the "baby" phase, it shows no control and urinates straight on to the parental body. But then, without any attempt at training from the foster-parent, the young animal suddenly one day gives warning. With a small grunt it thrusts itself away from the parent's body and, still clinging to it, urinates or defecates clear of it. The "hygiene" reaction seems to be completely instinctive and appears at a fixed point in their development, at somewhere around two years of age. In this respect, as in so many others, the human and ape infant are basically similar. The automatic cut-in of control mechanisms matures at certain stages and cannot easily be changed by training or artificial disciplines.

Why Do Most Mothers Cradle Their Babies in Their Left Arms?

One of the strangest features of motherhood is that the vast majority of mothers prefer to cradle their babies in their left arms. Why should this be? The obvious explanation is that the majority of mothers are right-handed and they wish to keep their right hands free. Unfortunately this explanation cannot apply, because left-handed mothers also favor their left arms for holding their babies. The precise figures are: 83 percent for right-handed and 78 percent for left-handed mothers.

The most likely explanation is that the mother's heart is on the left side and, by holding the baby in her left arm, she is unconsciously bringing her infant closer to the sound of the heartbeat. This is the sound that the baby heard when it was inside the mother's womb and which is therefore associated with peace, comfort, and security.

Tests were carried out in nurseries where some babies were played the recorded sound of a human heartbeat and, sure enough, those babies were lulled off to sleep twice as quickly as the others. We also know that the sound of the mother's heart is quite audible inside the womb and that the unborn baby has well developed hearing. The constant dull thud of the heart, beating so close to the fetus, second by second, must become the single most intrusive message from the outside world that a fetus can experience. So it is little wonder that traces of this imprinting appear later on, in babyhood.

It is interesting that fathers show less of this left-side bias than mothers, suggesting that the human female is better programmed for baby-carrying than her partner. Alternatively, she may be more sensitive to the mood of her baby and unconsciously adjusts her holding behavior to make her baby feel more secure.

Some new observations on our closest animal relatives, the chimpanzees and gorillas, have revealed that they too show a strong bias for left-side holding of their babies. The precise figures were 84 percent for chimpanzees and 82 percent for gorillas, remarkably close to the human percentage. Significantly, these apes do not show the strong right-handedness of the human species when using implements, which confirms the fact that left-holding has nothing to do with having a dominant right hand.

Recently a possible additional value in cradling babies on the left side has been suggested. It has been pointed out that, because the two sides of the brain are concerned with different aspects of behavior, it is possible that the mother, in cradling the baby to her left, is showing the baby her "best side." It is claimed that emotions are more strongly expressed on the left side of the human face and that she therefore gives the baby a better chance to read her emotional mood changes, as it gazes up at her. Furthermore, the mother's left eye and ear are more tuned in to emotional changes in her baby than her right eye and ear would be. So in addition to the baby seeing the more expressive part of its mother, there is the further advantage that the mother herself is more sensitive to the left-held baby. This may sound farfetched, but it is just possible that it could provide a slight, extra benefit for those mothers displaying the strange one-sided bias when cradling their infants.

How does the bias occur? Do the mothers have an instinctive preference for it, or do they learn it by trial and error, unconsciously adjusting the position of their babies until they are more calm? The surprising answer is that it seems to be the baby and not the mother who controls the bias. Observations of newborn infants when they were only a few hours old revealed that they come into the world with a pre-programmed tendency to turn their heads to the right. If the newborn's head is gently held in a dead central position and then released, it naturally swings to the right far more often than to the left. This happens in nearly 70 percent of babies. It means that when the mother goes to feed her infant, she finds its head more likely to turn that way and this may well influence her decision concerning which side is best for it. If it prefers turning its head to the right it will, of course, feel more at ease when it is held in the crook of her left arm. This will bring mother and baby more "face to face." This may only be part of the explanation because the holding bias is 80 percent and not 70 percent, but it adds a further intriguing chapter to the story.

How Do Babies
Learn to Talk?

Strictly speaking babies do not talk. The very name "infant" is taken from the Latin *infans* meaning "unable to speak." Nevertheless, babies are very vocal beings, even if they do not engage in true talking. The stream of sounds they love to make is called "babbling," and it goes through a number of characteristic stages during the first twelve months of life.

The very first stage makes hardly any noise at all, except for a faint bubbling sound. When only a month or two old, the baby can be observed to push its tongue out a little through its partly opened lips. It then brings its lips together and at the same time a little bubble of saliva emerges from the mouth. This can best be described as pre-babbling. The baby is mouthing the actions of vocalizing, coordinating its breathing with movements of its tongue and lips— the vital combination that will later provide the basis for speech. But as yet there is no sound to go with these movements.

Then, by the age of three months, the audible babbling begins and during the weeks ahead becomes something of an obsession. At first there are no more than experimental splutters and grunts, as though the baby is trying to blow raspberries at its parents. Then, as the weeks pass, open vowel sounds appear on the scene. This is the cooing phase, with rounded *ooo*s and *aaa*s becoming great favorites. Between the ages of three and six months this babbling becomes more and more frequent and often takes place when the baby is quite alone. It starts to add consonants to its vowel sounds, producing a variety of *ba, ka, da, ma, pa,* and *der* noises.

As the weeks pass the streams of babbling become more and more prolonged and complicated. They reach a crescendo at about six months of age and then subside slightly. This is because a new phase has been reached. In the old, simple babbling phase there was little or no relationship to other sounds being made by parents. If the baby said ma or pa it may have seemed like an identification to the mother or father, but it was not. It was simply vocal experimentation. Now, between six and seven months, several important new steps are taken. The single syllables are combined to produce such sounds as *mumum* and *dadad,* or *booboo* and *ala.* Again, parents may feel they have been identified, but for a while even these double syllables are made, not to them, but to the world in general.

Interaction does become more important, though. If parents talk to their babies at this age, the babies will pause in their babbling and listen. Also, they can identify a friendly voice even when they cannot see the speaker. And they may use vocalizing to attract attention, even though the precise sounds have no specific meanings. In addition, they begin to vary the volume, pitch, and rate at which they babble. In a sense they are rather like an orchestra that is tuning up, but has not yet started to play the music. That splendid moment may arrive at about the age of nine months, but only in a small percentage of babies. The majority are not so forward.

The first meaningful word is usually one directed to the parents, such as *mama,* or *dada.* Such sounds have been made before, but now, at last, they are directed at the real "moma" or "papa." At first it is only a matter of degree. The baby is observed to say *dada* more often in the presence of its father than when he is absent. Then, little by little, the word comes to *mean* father.

Three percent of children utter their first true word in this way by nine months; 10 percent by ten months; 50 percent by twelve months and 90 percent by eighteen months. By the age of one year many babies have mastered the use of several words, but it will take a further year before they can join words together spontaneously to make simple sentences.

Studies of babies born deaf reveal something important about baby talk. During the first six months of life, deaf babies babble just like all others, but then in the second six months their vocalizations go into a sharp decline. This tells us how important parents are in the second six months, with regard to the development of talking. At this phase it is clear that babies need to be talked to a great deal. They are interacting with their parents, even if they cannot immediately use words in specific contexts. Babies that have talkative parents do seem to learn much more easily to become good talkers themselves. They need the feedback of "conversations" with their mothers and fathers.

Some parents find themselves talking like their babies. Instead of helping their infants to imitate *them*, they imitate their infants. This has obvious shortcomings and yet it is amazing how many parents can be heard going coo-coo-coo to their babies, when they would be much better advised to talk normally—or even read to them. Normal adult speech contains a much richer variety of sounds and inflections and these can be heard by the babies even if they cannot copy them.

In fact, there is not a great deal of vocal imitation until toward the end of the first year of life. We know this because babies all over the world, from every culture and every language, produce the same kind of babble sounds. It is impossible to tell the babbling of a Japanese baby from that of a European or an American. So clearly, there is no significant degree of imitation taking place, whatever the parents may imagine. Only at the end of the first year, when real words begin to be spoken, do the language differences start to appear and to divide the babies from one another.

To answer the original question—How do babies learn to talk?— it seems that in the first six months of life they are all programmed to babble in the same way, deaf or hearing, Oriental or European. Then, in the second six months they are programmed to become sensitive to their parents and to listen carefully to their voices. A whole range of sounds is uttered, at first more or less randomly and then with each word being gradually restricted to one context or object.

So human babies do not really *learn* to talk at all. It is not something we teach them; it is an inborn characteristic of our species. We can encourage it by chatting to them and we can help them to refine it, but it is there inside every one of them. When they pass from babyhood to childhood our teaching can, of course, then become of increasing importance, but even at those later stages, there is more to talking than can be imparted by systematic teaching. There are a hundred million million million possible word combinations in the English language, we are told, and we certainly cannot learn to make sense of them by some form of schoolbook learning. We are "wired for speech" and it is perhaps the greatest of all our human attributes—one that starts out as a simple tongue and lip movement when we are only a few weeks out of the womb.

What Makes
Babies So Appealing?

When normal adults look at babies they feel uncontrollably protective toward them. These maternal and paternal feelings are inborn. They are built in to us genetically and require no learning or teaching. If certain unusual adults lack these feelings, then it means that they have somehow been traumatized and have had their natural parental responses damaged in some way. For them it is probably better not to have children because, if they do, they will transfer their problems on to their offspring and the traumas of loveless parent/offspring relations will continue to reverberate down the generations, causing untold emotional chaos in the process. It may be harsh to say it, but if an adult cannot look lovingly at a baby, it is preferable not to breed.

For those adults whose protective feelings have not been damaged, what is it exactly about a baby that makes it so appealing? We know the answer to this question because of a series of careful tests in which different features have been changed in pictures of babies and the adults' responsiveness to the different cases have been analyzed using involuntary emotional reactions such as pupil dilation. In other words, these tests have not relied on conscious verbal statements, but on unconscious reactions that cannot be "doctored," modified, improved, or concealed by the adults being examined.

In experiments of this kind it was found that the following aspects of "babyishness" have strong appeal for adults:

1. A large head in relation to the body
2. A large, prominent, bulbous forehead
3. Large eyes set low down on the face
4. Rounded, protruding cheeks
5. Short, heavy limbs, with clumsy movements
6. A general plumpness and roundedness of the body

These baby features are so powerful that their appeal still operates even when we come across them in other animals. This is why teddy bears and pandas are so appealing and so much more popular than other, more spindly species. It is also why dolls have such flat faces and why babyfaced adults have special "sex kitten" and "little-boy-lost" appeal in addition to their more usual sexual attractions.

For human babies these features are essential to survival, ensuring that their parents will want to take care of them, automatically and uncontrollably, even at times when the stresses of the day are bearing down upon them. And as such stresses do inevitably occur from time to time during early parenthood, human babies need all the assistance they can get from their ancient genetic inheritance.

Do Men and Women React Differently to the Sight of a Baby?

Yes, they do, but in a rather unexpected way, and it took special tests to prove it. The reason why it is not immediately obvious is because people are so polite. Asked if they like a particular baby, they usually respond enthusiastically to please its proud parents. But what are their true feelings?

The way to answer this question is to study the pupils of the eyes of the adults as they look at the baby. If they really do like what they see, they will show an unusual degree of pupil dilation, more than one might expect for the amount of light falling on their eyes. Even in bright light their pupils can be seen to expand slightly as they gaze at the infant in front of them. If they do *not* like what they see, despite their effusive words of praise, then their pupils will contract more than usual, as if they are trying to shut out the image of the object they are studying.

If the reactions of large numbers of adults are studied in this way, it emerges that people fall into two distinct categories: first, there are those that are themselves childless (whether married or single); second, there are those who already have children of their own. In both cases, the females show a massive, positive emotional response to the sight of a beautiful baby. Their pupils display a marked enlargement as they gaze fondly at its form.

With males, however, there is a fascinating difference. Men who already have children of their own also show a strong positive response, with almost as much pupil enlargement as the females. But men who have yet to become fathers, whether single or married, show a strong *negative* response, their pupils shrinking as if to shut out the picture of the baby before them.

These results reveal that the parental feelings of human males and females operate differently. Young females come ready-primed for maternal behavior, while young males must have it activated within them by the presence of their own babies. This does not mean that human males are bad parents. It simply indicates that, for them, the protective, parental urges require external arousal, whereas with the human females there is an automatic self-arousal from an early stage.

This is less alarming for young women than it may at first appear. It shows that the young adult male who takes little interest in other people's babies may turn out to be a much more devoted father of his own infant than one might think on the earlier evidence.

Why Do Some Mothers Have Twins?

In European countries and in the United States the chance of producing twins is about 1 in 100. This is not true everywhere. In parts of Japan, for instance, the figure is as low as 1 in 200, and in parts of Africa, such as Nigeria, it is as high as 1 in 22.

So it would seem that racial background plays a part in determining how likely a mother is to deliver twin babies. It could be argued against this that it is differences in climate rather than racial factors that cause the cultural variations, but the evidence is against this. For example, in Great Britain black immigrant mothers remain more likely than Asian, Indian, or Japanese immigrant mothers to produce twins, despite the fact that they all suffer equally from the rigors of the British climate.

A closer look at the kinds of twins produced shows that the racial variations all apply to non-identical twins. The likelihood of having identical twins remains more or less constant all over the globe, at a rate of only 3 or 4 per 1,000 births.

Non-identical twins, by contrast, do seem to be influenced by a number of factors. In addition to racial differences, there are a number of personal ones. The chances of having non-identical twins are increased if the mother has already had twins before, is herself a twin, or if she has brothers or sisters who are twins. These factors shorten the odds from 100 to 1 to 70 to 1. The presence of *identical* twins in the family history makes no difference whatever. Nor does the presence of non-identical twins on the father's side of the family.

The mother's age also influences the chance of having non-identical twins. The older she is, the greater the chance. By her late thirties she has again reduced her odds from 100 to 1 to 70 to 1. The other main factor is the size of the family. The more children she has already had, the greater the chance of having twins next time, regardless of her age.

Bigger women are also more prone to twinning. If they are taller or fatter than average, they are more likely to give birth to a pair of twins than if they are slim and petite.

Affluence begets twins. During wartime the records showed a decrease in twinning alongside the decrease in the quality of food available. After the Second World War there was a sudden twin-boom, with the figure in Europe rising to 1 in 80. Similar changes are known in animals and this is clearly adaptive. When food is scarce female animals have smaller litters; when it is plentiful they have larger litters.

The production of non-identical twins is the result of the female shedding not her usual one egg, but two at once, which are fertilized by different sperm, in contrast to identical twins, where a single egg divides in two after it has been fertilized. From the great rarity of twins compared with single births, it is obvious that the reproductive "intention" or plan of our species is to have only one child at a time. Even single human babies put such heavy demands on their mothers that this makes a great deal of sense. So having twins is, in a way, a mistake—a minor inefficiency of the system. This may explain why it is that women who are slightly more likely to have twins are a little plumper than average, a little older than average mothers, better fed than average, more fecund than average, and so on.

It seems that certain kinds of sexual behavior may increase the chances of having twins. In general it can be said that when the sexual behavior at conception is more sudden, more passionate, or more violent, twinning is more frequent. We know, for instance, that twins are more likely to arrive when the mother is a new bride, is the wife of a returning soldier or sailor following a long absence, is unmarried, or is raped. In all these cases the mating act is more likely to be an intensely emotional experience and it may be this that triggers the extra egg.

Against all these social factors, there are personal genetic factors as well, with increased twinning occurring in certain family lines. In such instances, none of the social factors mentioned above may apply. And in *all* cases, the chances of having twins remain very low when compared with a single baby.

To sum up, the best chance for a man to become the father of twins is to marry a tall, overweight, thirty-seven-year-old Nigerian woman who has twin sisters and twin brothers and to make passionate love to her on the honeymoon. At a rough guess that should increase the chances of fathering twins to about 10 to 1.

The record for multiple births goes to a Russian peasant woman who is reputed to have produced no fewer than sixteen pairs of twins, seven sets of triplets, and four sets of quadruplets, back in the eighteenth century. With the side-effects of various modern fertility drugs creating more and more big "litters" of babies today, we may yet see her record broken, but for the average woman the risk of experiencing record-breaking in this particular form of contest is remote. Even a single set of triplets is only an 8,000 to 1 chance, and beyond that the odds become infinitesimally small.

Why Do Babies Cry in Airplanes?

Mothers flying with small babies are often pleasantly surprised at how contentedly they slumber the miles away. Then, as the captain begins his descent to land, the peace is shattered by inconsolable crying. The baby starts screaming in acute distress and nothing seems to calm it. Why should this be?

The answer lies in a small, air-filled cavity of the middle ear, a space about 8 millimeters by 4 millimeters, which must for comfort always be at the same air pressure as the outside world. As the aircraft descends, this balance of pressure is temporarily lost and the result can be quite painful, especially in the case of a baby, whose ears are anatomically more delicate, and who cannot understand the sharp aching sensation that is suddenly throbbing inside its head.

Adults can relieve their own pain by pinching the nose, pursing the lips tight, and blowing hard. This drives air up the eustachian tubes that connect the cavities of the middle ears with the back of the throat, and redresses the imbalance in pressure. But parents cannot help the baby in this way, and must wait for the slower adjustment that will eventually follow without any special aids.

Experienced mothers, who fly a great deal and who anticipate this problem, attempt to solve it by starting to feed the baby from a bottle just before the descent begins. This is by no means infallible, but it does seem to soothe some babies, and is certainly worth trying.

Why Are Babies Circumcised?

Millions of male babies, all over the world, suffer the strange mutilation of having their foreskins removed within a few days of birth. In some countries this is done within a few hours of delivery. In others it is delayed until the third or fourth day after delivery. In still others it takes place on the eighth day.

Before asking why it is done, what are the facts of the operation itself? It involves the surgical removal of the skin that protects the sensitive tip of the penis from friction, infection, and physical damage. It is not a useless appendage to be casually discarded, but a valuable part of the human male anatomy. At birth it is attached to the underlying skin and cannot be retracted. It does not become loose until the child is three or four years old, and it is a mistake to attempt to pull it back on a male baby, as this can damage the tissue.

When the foreskin is cut away it causes the baby considerable pain and leaves an exposed patch that has to be covered with a dressing. There is a serious risk of infection or bleeding. This is not a rare occurrence. A recent study revealed that 22 percent of circumcised babies suffered from either hemorrhage or some kind of sepsis. Also, the exposed opening at the end of the penis is at risk, especially from wet diapers, and frequently develops ulcers. In Great Britain alone, there are on average sixteen deaths a year as a result of this "minor" operation.

Given these facts, why is it done? If we were to mutilate male babies in any other way, we would be prosecuted for child abuse. How has circumcision survived into the twentieth century? To find the answer we have to go back six thousand years. It started as an ancient Egyptian custom and there are wall carvings to prove it. It seems to have its origin in snake worship. The Egyptians believed that when the snake shed its skin, and emerged shiny and new again, it was undergoing rebirth. They reasoned that if, by shedding skin, the snake could become apparently immortal, then humans should follow suit. They made the simple equation: snakeskin = foreskin, and the operation began. From there it spread to many Semitic peoples, both Arabs and Jews adopting it and converting it into an act of religious faith. As the centuries passed it became popular in other regions of the world for moral, medical, or hygienic reasons, and it is still performed today on millions of babies all over the globe.

Apart from the original superstitious reasons, it has been said to be valuable because: (1) It limits intercourse. (2) It provides a badge of tribal or social allegiance. (3) It makes men holy because the prophet Mohammed was born without a foreskin. (4) It is unclean to have a foreskin. (5) It prevents masturbation. (6) It provides an offering to the gods in the form of a symbol of the male virility. (7) It removes a physical defect from the male body. (8) The Devil hides beneath the foreskin, and therefore to remove this skin is to remove his hiding place and expose him. (9) The foreskin caused many medical conditions such as hysteria, epilepsy, and nocturnal incontinence. (10) The foreskin caused mental illness. (11) The foreskin caused cancer of the penis in males and cancer of the cervix in their wives. (12) Its removal makes a boy grow up to "feel regular."

All these reasons are complete nonsense. There is not a single valid argument in favor of mutilating baby boys in this way. The truth in each case is as follows: (1) Circumcision has no effect, one way or the other, on the sexual performance of the adult male. (2) It no longer provides a mark of allegiance because it has been carried out on such a wide range of males from so many cultures and societies in different parts of the world. (3) Mohammed may well have been born without a foreskin. This is a condition that is well known to science, but to imitate it is hardly a formula for making men holy. (4) It is not unclean to have a foreskin providing the adult male washes beneath it from time to time—an easy enough task today. (5) It has no effect whatever on masturbation rates. (6) Since foreskin removal does not decrease male virility, it is a poor offering to make to the gods. (7) It does not remove a physical defect, but a valuable physical attribute—a protective fold of skin. (8) Those who believe in the Devil know perfectly well that he can enter the human body through any unprotected orifice, which makes the circumcised individual more vulnerable than the uncircumcised. (9) The foreskin causes no medical weaknesses of any kind, but does prevent some, as already mentioned. (10) The foreskin causes no form of mental illness. (11) Claims that it causes cancer have now been revealed as completely false. (12) If it "makes a boy feel regular" to be mutilated in this way, then we are back to the primitive condition of tribal scarring that, in every other aspect, we now find abhorrent.

There is another, rather unpleasant, reason for male circumcision being carried out in modern times. In some countries, babies are treated in this way because it provides an attractive fee for the doctors who perform the operation. Significantly, in Britain, where a National Health Service removed the doctor's fee, the frequency of the operation fell to 0.41 percent of the male population. In another country, where the fees were still in force, over 80 percent of male babies were circumcised before they left the maternity hospitals.

The plain fact is that circumcision is a form of "child care" that male babies can well do without. Female babies are more fortunate. Their bodies are less suitable for mutilation and they are able to pass through their babyhood without genital wounding. Unhappily this does not mean they will always escape later on. For many young girls, in no fewer than twenty-five different countries, circumcision is performed even today. The fact that they are past the baby stage makes it worse, because they are more aware of what is happening to them. In some countries the clitoris alone is removed, but in others the mutilation is even more severe. There are today sadly no fewer than 74 million women who have been subjected to circumcision in Africa, the Middle East, and parts of Asia.

Why Are
Babies Baptized?

Many people associate baptism with the Christian practice of naming a child at a christening ceremony, but baptism is a much older ritual, performed for thousands of years in many cultures all over the world. Essentially it is the purification of the newborn child with water.

If so many adults in so many places and so many epochs have been determined to purify the newborn, it follows that they must have considered it impure in the first place. Why should this be? Why on earth should such a totally innocent being, fresh from the womb, be viewed as "impure"? To a rational mind this does not make sense, but there is nothing rational about baptism. It is a strange relic of earlier times, when adult life was plagued with superstition and magical spells.

There are two explanations for the supposed impurity of the newborn. In the first, the act of birth is seen as essentially "animalistic" and the baby is viewed as a small creature full of the evil qualities supposed to reside in animals. To raise it to a higher plain—to humanize it—something must be done. By dipping it in water, or sprinkling it with water, it is made pure simply because of the purity of the water itself. This symbolically cleanses it of its animal qualities and *makes* it innocent.

The second explanation sees the newborn, not so much as inherently evil, but as potentially evil. Because the baby is such a vulnerable, unprotected being and because the birth is such a happy event, it was supposed that this would attract evil spirits who would attach themselves to the baby if it was not rendered resistant in some way. Evil spirits were well known for arriving in force shortly after something special had happened to a human being. Moments of good fortune were particularly appealing to them. So the pure water treatment was administered to make the baby strong and to safeguard it against the bombardment of evil forces. Failure to baptize the baby would mean that evil spirits would enter its body and control it for the rest of its life.

There have been some curious variants on the baptism ceremony. In Ireland in the sixteenth century it was felt that a male baby's right arm—badly needed in adult life to put his enemies to the sword and the dagger, should remain impure. The right arms of babies were therefore kept carefully dry at the moment of baptism. These infants could then grow up pure in heart and body, but evil in their right arms, which would become their instrument of adult death and destruction.

The reactions of the baby to being baptized were thought to be important. In some societies the baby had to cry, in others it had to remain silent, if all was to be well in later life. The Christian baby was expected to bawl its head off, because this explosive crying action was the infant's way of expelling the evil spirits that were trying to enter its body. Other cultures see crying as the baby's resistance to purification and conclude that a crying baby at baptism is one that the demons will claim at an early age. For those who do not take such matters seriously, but who still wish to have their baby baptized as an act of social conformity, and as an excuse for a celebration of a new family addition, there is the comfort that, whether the infant cries or is silent, there is an optimistic interpretation available for both circumstances.

Why Are Baby Boys Dressed in Blue and Baby Girls in Pink?

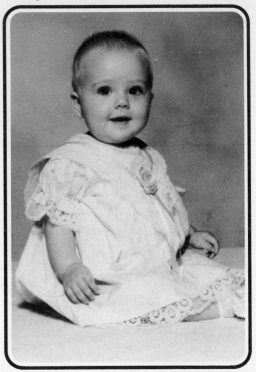

The answer to this question will not please the modern woman. The practice dates back to ancient times, when baby boys were thought to be greatly superior to baby girls. For them, a special protective color was needed, ensuring that they would flourish. Blue was chosen because it was the color of the heavens and therefore offered heavenly protection against the powers of evil.

In those days the belief in the existence of evil spirits was widespread and intense. These malevolent forces were thought to be especially attracted to times and places of great human joy, such as birth, marriage, and moments of triumph and success. So it was at these times that special actions were needed to ward off the attacks of the imagined spirit-powers. A whole range of superstitions developed over the centuries and, although we no longer believe in evil spirits, we still wish one another "good luck" and try to avoid "bad luck," and we continue to perform many of the ancient protective rituals, such as crossing our fingers, wearing something borrowed when getting married, carrying the bride over the threshold, and avoiding walking under ladders. All these actions have secret, forgotten meanings and they help to protect us from the ancient, evil spirits. So it is with dressing male babies in "heavenly" blue, the color of the sky, where the forces of good reside in their majestic domain.

If the evil spirits gather menacingly around the new baby's nursery, trying to enter and do the infant harm, they will be held in check and driven back by the magical powers of the sacred blue color of the young one's clothing and the other decorations in the room. In some countries in the Middle East, the whole house is protected rather than just the babies, by the painting of the front door a bright blue.

If blue clothing was a necessary form of insurance against supernatural assault, it seems rather strange not to have provided baby girls with a similar protection. Why not dress them in blue too? The practical answer was that it was useful to have an immediately visible distinction between the male and female infants. So some kind of non-blue color was essential. The choice of pink appears to have been made because this is the color of the baby's skin (in ancient Europe, at least). It is earthy and biological for the female body, in contrast with the ethereal, celestial blue of the young males. Psychologically, pink is associated with healthiness and cleanness—the pure pink of the unblemished skin—and this gives it an added appeal as the symbolic color of the female baby. Pink may not possess the protective values of blue, but then, if female babies were thought of as so inferior to males, why would the evil spirits have any interest in them? They did not need any special protection, merely an appropriate label to distinguish them from their male companions.

As centuries passed and the original reasons for blue and pink adornments were forgotten, new explanations had to be invented to answer the inevitable queries. It was stated that boys wore blue because male babies were born in blue cabbage patches, and that girls wore pink because they were born inside pink roses. Later still, these fanciful explanations were forgotten and, in present times, few people have any knowledge of the meanings of the baby color symbolisms. But as with so many superstitions, the forgetting of the origin of a belief does little to stop its progression from generation to generation. Blue for a boy and pink for a girl simply becomes an accepted "custom" and is followed without question.

Why Was the Baby's Arrival Celebrated with a Birthday Cake?

At the party to celebrate the baby's safe arrival—the christening party or its equivalent—it has in the past been a widespread custom to display a special birthday cake. A similar cake reappears at each anniversary of the birthday, accompanied by a small ritual, but few involved know the true significance of what they are doing. Without realizing it, they are performing an ancient form of moon worship. This is why the typical birthday cake is circular in shape, white in color, and lit with candles. The circular design copies the shape of the full moon, the white icing suggests the pale color of the moon, and the flames of the candles symbolize the moonlight.

This custom began in ancient Greece, when worshipers made offerings to the moon goddess in the form of small, circular cakes, each lit with a single candle. The idea of celebrating a birthday was borrowed by the Greeks from the ancient Egyptians, and the use of confectionery from the ancient Persians.

In the Middle Ages, German peasants elaborated the custom, lighting candles at dawn and keeping them alight all day, until they were ceremonially blown out at the evening gathering, when the cake was shared out and eaten. The candles had to be extinguished with a single breath if a secret wish, made at the same moment, was to come true. The newborn baby's birthday cake had only one candle. At the end of babyhood, when the infant was one year old, it had two candles, and then another was added for each additional year of life, at each subsequent anniversary of the birth.

In modern times we have made the error of ignoring the "birth candle." A one-year-old infant celebrates its first birthday with one candle, a two-year-old with two candles, and so on, but this is wrong. There should always be one more candle than the number of years. This is because the first candle—the single candle of the original "birth cake" should be added each year. It is the Candle of Life and symbolizes the child's arrival and existence as a living being.

As with so many ceremonial uses of fire, there is a magical element in the presence of the birthday cake candles. Their burning light is meant to repel the evil spirits that are always attracted to moments of human celebration. That is why they must be formally extinguished at the end of a birthday party—to show that the event has passed off successfully and that their protection is no longer needed. Since they also symbolize life, the act of blowing them out with one breath is to display a complete and efficient control over the forces of life. It demonstrates a momentary ability to control one's own destiny, which is why a secret wish for the future, made at the same moment, will come true.

All this begins with the original birthday cake when, if you believe in magical powers, you should provide the newborn with a circular, white cake lit with a single Candle of Life, should make a silent wish for its future happiness, and then, on its behalf, blow out the candle to complete the ancient ritual.

Why Was the Stork Said to Bring Babies?

When babies were born in the home rather than in the maternity hospital, the other children in the family became intensely curious and demanded to know where the new baby had come from and why their mother was lying in bed, as if sick or injured. Instead of telling them the truth, parents invented a story to explain the sudden arrival and the mother's weakness. They told the children that a stork had delivered the baby and that, when it handed it over to the mother, it pecked the mother's leg and made it bleed. This conveniently explained the suddenness of the baby's arrival, the fact that the mother had to stay in bed, and even the presence of blood-stained linen. Children accepted this explanation and it spread worldwide as a simple and popular legend. But why the stork?

The legend began in those parts of Europe where, each year, storks nested on the roofs of houses, especially in Germany, Holland, and parts of Scandinavia. There it was noted that these huge birds, big enough and strong enough to be able to carry heavy weights—such as a newborn baby—returned each season to precisely the same rooftops as before. Many householders started to erect special platforms on their roofs, to encourage the storks to nest there. During the day, the storks went off to hunt for food in the nearby streams, lakes, and marshes—precisely the places where the souls of unborn children were thought to dwell. So it was easy for them to find the babies there and carry them back to their nesting places, where they could deliver them down the chimneys and into the parental bedrooms. The fact that storks were seen to be extremely good parents with their own offspring, and to care for their chicks with great devotion and tenderness, made them even more suitable as candidates for delivering human babies.

If it seems strange to think of inventing the delivery of a baby from elsewhere to the mother's bedroom, it is worth recalling that in earlier times there was a widespread belief in the great Mother Goddess, or Earth Mother, who was thought to be responsible for giving birth to *all* nature, including human babies. She was supposed to produce the new infants from her own body—the earth itself—and place them there for humans (and other animals) to find. Sometimes parents told their children that they had simply discovered the new babies in a "cabbage patch," "under a gooseberry bush," or some other such place, lying on the earth where the great Earth Mother had deposited them.

Bearing this in mind, the stork in the legend becomes no more than a convenient messenger, saving the human mother the trouble of going out to look for her new baby—a fair exchange for the valuable nest-site supplied by the mother's house.

When a Baby Is Hurt, Why Do We "Kiss It to Make It Better"?

W hen a baby has reached the stage of vigorous crawling and is starting to bump into sharp objects, it often bangs itself hard enough to make it cry. The mother's typical reaction is to go to the infant, pick it up, and cuddle it, at the same time examining the spot that was hit for cuts or bruising. In addition to hugging it, she may also rock it in her arms and pat its back, cooing softly to it. This usually calms the baby and the interaction is very likely to end with the mother asking "where it hurts" and then kissing the spot that she considers to be the site of the injury. As she performs this kiss, she can often be heard to say to the infant, "let's kiss it and make it better."

Applying her lips to the injured spot has no physical or medical value whatsoever, and yet it is curiously comforting, both to her and her offspring. This is partly due to the reassuring performance of a gentle intimacy, but there is more to it than that. The mother is in fact carrying out an ancient magical practice, symbolically sucking out the "evil forces" that are supposedly causing the pain. In earlier centuries, there would have been a more explicit attempt to suck out the pain, with the lips applying suction to the damaged spot. But over the years the true meaning of "kiss and make it better" has been forgotten and a simple, loving kiss now replaces the witchdoctor's powerful sucking action.

Why Does the Proud Father Hand Out Cigars When His Baby Is Born?

The widespread custom of handing out cigars to his male friends when a man becomes a father has an unusual origin. It is an invitation to the men to share in the sending of thanks to the ancient gods in the heavens above. If this sounds fanciful, it is only because we have forgotten the original function of smoking, which was essentially religious. The smoke from the cigars is intended to waft away and rise up to the heavens where it enters the nostrils of the gods and communicates to them the celebration that is taking place down below. It is, in other words, a fragrant way of giving thanks to the gods for the safe delivery of the new baby.

The ancient Mayans appear to have been the first people to have blown smoke at the heavens in this way. In their case, worshiping a sun god, it was a comparatively simple matter to direct their clouds of smoke toward the sun in the sky above. From them, the religious use of tobacco seems to have spread widely through the Americas. We all know, if only from the cinema, the North American Indian habit of sharing a "peace pipe," which was just one of the sacred ceremonies that developed from the Mayan tradition. Ceremonial group smoking of this kind is still found in many men's clubs throughout the world today, when adult males who perhaps never smoke at other times, indulge in the cosy ritual of filling a dining room with cigar smoke following a formal dinner. The religious origins of the actions are no longer remembered, but the sense of shared fire-making has about it a special, magical quality. It is this that the proud father is symbolically rekindling when he hands out the traditional cigars to his friends.

The question remains: Why cigars and not cigarettes? Two explanations have been offered. The first sees the cigars as no more than "expensive cigarettes," and their use as demonstration of the need for the new father to share his good fortune. This is the tribal "potlatch" tradition, where someone who is better off than his companions makes a lavish sacrifice as a way of reducing envy. The new father, suddenly blessed with the great gift of a child, must make an extravagant gesture—hence the expensive cigars.

The second explanation is a simple Freudian one that sees the cigars as phallic symbols—"erect" cigarettes that advertise his virility, the virility that led to this moment . . . the birth of his offspring.

In the new, health-conscious, post-tobacco era it will be interesting to see what new form of proud-father display replaces the carcinogenic luxuries of the traditional past.

Why Is a Baby
Called a Baby?

T he newborn human was originally referred to as a *baban*. This was then shortened to *babe* and babe in turn was modified to *baby*. The shift from baban to babe to baby is similar to changes in personal names such as Thomas to Tom to Tommy, or Nicola to Nick to Nicky. But although we think of Tommy and Nicky as informal pet names, the word baby has lost that quality and become the formal term for the newborn. Its predecessor, babe, is now only used in biblical or poetic contexts, and baban has not been in common use for over seven hundred years.

All three of these names for the newborn offspring, along with variants such as bab, baba, babi, babee, babby, babie, babye, babbon, and the French bébé, owe their origin to the same source—namely the first strong sound made by the child when it reaches an age of three to four months and starts to utter open vowels. These vowel sounds begin as *aaa*s and *ooo*s, reminiscent of the cooing of a dove. Then consonants are added and out of the confusion of earlier babbling and gurgling there suddenly appears to have emerged something like a word. Three consonants are favored at the very beginning of this great step forward in vocal communication: B, M, and P. Combined with the aaa sound they create three key utterances—baa, maa, and paa. It is no accident that these three first "words" of the baby have become designated as the "titles" of the three most important people in its life—itself, its mother, and its father—the baa becoming *baba*, the maa *mama*, and the paa *papa*. This simple act of repetition forms the three key words that it learns to use before any others. Which name was applied to which individual was originally probably arbitrary, but once the B, the M, and the P consonants were linked to the child, the mother, and the father respectively, there was no turning back.

Index

Overpopulation, 159
Overstimulation, 75

Pacifiers. *See* Artificial nipples
Pain, 74
Parallelogram skull, 35
Parental recognition, 51
Parents. *See* Fathers; Mothers
Paternal instincts, 182
Pelvis, 8, 32
Perambulator. *See* Baby carriage
Personal fragrance, 59–60, 101–102
Pink (color), 198
Placenta, 22–23
Play, 129–133
Port wine stains, 38
Postnatal depression, 122
Pre-milk. *See* Colostrum
Pressure marks (birthmark), 36
Primary teeth, 44
Protein, 104
Pupils, 39–41

Rag mother, 82
   see also Mother substitute
Rapid eye movement. *See* REM-sleep
Rattles, 130
Reference person. *See* Mother-figure
Reflex smile, 86–87
REM-sleep, 125
Reward. *See* Magnified reward
Right-handed bias, 150–156
Rocking, 166–167
Room temperature, 71–72
Rooting, 94
Routine feeding, 97

Schedule feeding, 97
Sebaceous glands, 19, 28
Security. *See* Insecurity
Security blankets. *See* Mother substitutes
Self-rocking, 167
Skull, 32–35
Sleep
   duration, 117–118
   location, 119–123
   REM, 125
Smell (sense), 59–61
Smiling, 86–89
Smoking, ceremonial, 208
Soft spots. *See* Fontanelles
Sound localization, 56–57

Specific smile, 86, 87–88
Speech. *See* Talking
Spider marks (birthmark), 37
Startle reflex, 56, 67, 87
Sterilization (bottle), 101
Stimulation, 148–149
Stork bites (birthmark), 36–37
Storks, 203–204
Stranger anxiety, 51, 87–88
Strawberry marks, 37–38
Stress chemicals, 84–85
Sucking, 93–96
Sugar, 104
Sutures (skull), 34
Swaddling, 121, 161–165
Swaddling board, 169
Sweat glands, 69
Swimming, 140–144
Symmetry (skull), 33, 35

Talking, 57–58, 178–181
Taste (sense), 62–64
Tear ducts, 84
Teeth, 42–44
Teething pain, 44
Temperature, body. *See* Body temperature
Testicles, 31
Thumb sucking, 93
Toilet-training, 171–174
Tonic neck reflex, 155
Toys, 133
Transitional comfort objects. *See* Mother
   substitutes
Triplets, 189
Twins, 186–189

Umbilical cord, 15–16, 21–22, 23
Understimulation, 75
Urbanization, 121

Vernix caseosa, 16, 19–20, 28
Victoria, Queen, 169
Vision, 48–52
Vocal imitation, 55, 180

Walking, 137–139
Water births, 143–144
Water-logging, 19
Weaning, 107–110
Weeping, 83–85

Yawning, 24–26